THE BIG BLACK THING

CHAPTER. 2

Edited by
Michael Mohammed Ahmad
and Winnie Dunn

Aboriginal and Torres Strait Islander writing edited by
Ellen van Neerven

First published in 2018
from the Writing and Society Research Centre
at Western Sydney University
by Sweatshop: Western Sydney Literacy Movement
Bankstown Campus, Building 3, Room G.42
Locked Bag 1797, Penrith NSW 2751
www.sweatshop.ws
Text copyright © to the authors
Printed and bound by McPherson's Printing Group
Cataloguing-in-Publication data is available from the
National Library of Australia
ISBN 978-0-9924886-7-3 (paperback)

WRITING AND SOCIETY
RESEARCH CENTRE

Acknowledgements

This project has been an initiative of Sweatshop: Western Sydney Literacy Movement in partnership with WestWords: Western Sydney's Literature Development Organisation and the Western Sydney University Writing and Society Research Centre.

This project is supported by the NSW Government through Create NSW, and the Crown Resorts Foundation and Packer Family Foundation, and Western Sydney University.

Production Team

Editors / Michael Mohammed Ahmad and Winnie Dunn

Editor: Aboriginal and Torres Strait Islander Writing / Ellen van Neerven

Assistant Editor / Shirley Le: 2017 WestWords Western Sydney Emerging Writers' Fellow

Layout and Design / Nadine Beyrouti and Elaine Lim

School Workshop Facilitators / Winnie Dunn, Ellen van Neerven, Shirley Le, Mariam Cheik-Hussein, Louisa Badayala, Tamar Chnorhokian, Khalid Warsame and Michael Mohammed Ahmad

Special Thanks / Michael Campbell, Executive Director, WestWords / Anthony Uhlmann, Director, Western Sydney University Writing and Society Research Centre / Anne McLean, Manager, Schools Engagement, Western Sydney University / Jacqui Cornforth, Pathways to Dreaming Project Officer, Western Sydney University / Josh Mason, Pathways to Dreaming Project Officer, Western Sydney University / Kate Clarkson, Creative Arts EAL/D Teacher, Lurnea IEC and High School / Helen Lee, Head Teacher, Lurnea IEC / Andrea Soto, Refugee Support Officer, Lurnea High School / Ahmed Ibrahim, Student, Lurnea High School / Omar Al Lahibi, Student, Lurnea High School / Maha Adler, Head Teacher English, Languages and EAL/D, Sir Joseph Banks High School / Dionissia Tsirigos, Head Teacher English, Wiley Park Girls High School / Fatma Akkawi, English/HSIE Teacher, Wiley Park Girls High School / Augusta Supple, Senior Manager, Engagement, Partnerships and Development, Create NSW

Foreword

People always assume that the title of our anthology means something perverse. 'The Big Black Thing? More like my big black shit!' one high school student smirked as the boys howled with laughter.

Jokes aside, The Big Black Thing always captures attention wherever it is presented. The title was originally borrowed from an Instagram caption written by lina Kastoumis, which featured in Chapter. 1. Now the title of our anthology series is more like a metaphor for Sweatshop's version of contemporary Australian literature, which carries and reclaims stories written by marginalised people from Indigenous and culturally and linguistically diverse backgrounds.

The Big Black Thing: Chapter. 1 was launched at Walsh Bay for the Sydney Writers' Festival in May 2017. We invited every contributor to take part in the celebration and enter a privileged literary space previously closed off to most minority communities from Western Sydney. Our writers travelled from Bankstown, Blacktown, Parramatta, Mt Druitt, Penrith, Auburn and Liverpool to participate. It was a full house. Right when the doors closed, young refugee writers from Lurnea High School knocked on the windows trying to get into their own event. With every seat taken, those of us from Sweatshop chanted, 'Let Them In!' The organisers eventually violated fire safety codes just for us to stop yelling. This is how I've seen The Big Black Thing attempt to transform literature and lives: It has opened doors to showcase writing that pushes back against racist, sexist, classist and queerphobic narratives produced in Australia and around the world by mainstream media, art and television. As author and feminist Chimamanda Ngozi Adichie argues, when the marginalised write against, beyond and despite dangerous single narratives, we create awareness, multiplicity and original contributions to world knowledge.

Weaved into this second issue of The Big Black Thing are new and familiar writers from the Western Sydney Writers Group, who have reclaimed their hybrid identities through prose and poetry. Shirley Le and Stephen Pham remember Auburn-born, Myuran Sukumaran, a member of the Bali Nine who was executed in 2015 by the Indonesian Government for drug trafficking. Monikka Eliah finds her nana in a knitted jumper, Peter Polites examines the relationship between local and international violence against queer men of colour, Tamar Chnorhokian shows us what it means to be a 'sik bitch' and Gabby Florek reveals the 'Brown hand of God' in her Afro Peruvian ancestry. Amanda Yeo writes about the awkward stumbles and casual puns in flirting, Adam Anderson speaks to the diaspora of being a mixed-raced Indonesian man in his ancestral homeland, Samantha Hogg fights off her inner demons with a sprained ankle and Tien Tran brings the suburbs of Perth to the doorstep of Western Sydney in a 'stupid-ass' orange car. Once again, there is also an exciting collection of poetry from the Western Sydney Writers Group featured in The Big Black Thing: Omar Sakr spills Arab identity across Lurnea, Kane Harrington re-introduces us to the might of the pen, Jason Gray street talks from above and Evelyn Araluen maps out Dodge City, lined with goanna trees, COSTCO and Macca's.

Alongside these contributions are the works of young writers from Sir Joseph Banks High School, Lurnea High School and Wiley Park Girls High School. Students from first, second and third generation Arab, African, East Asian, South Asian, South-East Asian and Pasifika backgrounds take readers through the burnt rubber roads of the Hume Highway to midnight gunfire in the streets of Baghdad.

The pages within this book also include a series of untitled works by young Aboriginal and Torres Strait Islander writers from Glenmore Park High School, Kingswood High School and St Clair High School. This particular content was curated and edited by award-winning Yugambeh author Ellen van Neerven, and the stories of First Nation Australians speak for themselves loud and clear.

Lastly, The Big Black Thing: Chapter. 2 is blessed with six artworks from this year's feature artist, Emma Hicks. I first met Emma at a Sweatshop picnic in 2017 and immediately came to admire her empathy for mundane phenomena. I remember Emma alerting me to a small common myna bird lying in the dirt of Auburn Botanic Gardens. We thought it died until it rustled its feathers and flew upward. This is what Emma's collection of artworks, titled 'Conversations: feathers, quandongs and tracks', reminds me of – using ink to cast footprints, seedlings and feathers, she has created conversations about responsibilities, ethics and stories in the places we inhabit.

Even in the year 2018, Australia remains a country that seems to lack the kind of mainstream literature which reflects the colour of our history and modern society. Here again, in the pages ahead, is a collection of prose and poetry that go against, beyond and despite a mono-cultural version of Australia. Here again is this big black thing...

Winnie Dunn / Sweatshop Manager and Editor

Table of Contents

Table of Contents

Table of Contents

Table of Contents

Table of Contents

Talk Shit

Auckland Uati

—

Don't fuck with a Samoan lady. They always have a fire under their bellies just waiting to get lit. Samoan families talk shit. One time my cousin Paulo said, 'We bought a new PS4 today.' Even though he didn't. Mum rubbed her belly and said with big eyes, 'Ohh we bought that ages ago.' We didn't have shit. We never have shit.

Dark, Putrid Lines

Marko Poletanovic

/ The Meet

I arrived at the car park at Centro late as usual of course. My friends were already there with their JDMs all organised, prepped and ready for the race. We took it down to the Hume Highway just past the reservoir. Two paved lines of the traffic-plagued road were about to receive a couple more sets of tyres. We each lined up at the lights: Suly in his RX7, Toey in his 2JZ, Jaaf in his R32, Fouf in his STI, and me in my R34 Skyline. The lights shortly after like half an hour, turned green. The windows of nearby shook, and the road was rumbling. Us boys scarred dark, putrid lines and tyre smoke on the road, and floored it down the highway, quickly approaching 100/mph.

/ Krispy Kreme

I was in my Twin Turbo Supra as I clocked 187/mph on the Hume Highway. The coppers pulled me over to the side of the road and straight away a tall fat shit gets out of the car and comes to my window. I had a twelve pk of Krispy Kreme glazed donuts on the lap of some chick in the passenger seat.

'Do you know why I pulled you over?' said the fat copper with a bogan as accent.

'Cause you smelt my Krispy Kreme, didn't ya?'

Bankstown's National Anthem

Paris Caroline Henry

———

It was 3am on a Friday night. Never and I repeat never, trust any idea you have on a Friday night at 3am, trust me. My legs were crossed, sitting in front of my bedroom mirror, wearing my finest Winnie the Pooh pyjamas. My green curls struggled for freedom against a black hair tie on its last life. I tucked a loose strand behind my ear.

'Maybe I should pierce my own ear tonight… nah that's a bad id—' I heard the piercing, shrieking sirens of police cars, Bankstown's National Anthem.

So I was sitting here wearing rubber sink gloves. In one hand, I held the needle that, in my 3am haze, was sterilised with hand sanitiser. In the other was a rubber, yes a rubber, which I was holding behind my ear in order to stabilise it. You know, when other people have an existential crisis they buy a car or sneak out of home. Nope not me though. Maybe I shouldn't be so cheap and get this done professionally. Naaaaah. In my last attempt at making this as pain free as possible, I covered my ears in Bonjela, you know, the stuff used to numb babies' gums during teething, yup, it's as dumb as it sounds.

My hands were shaking, 'Come on Paris, you can do this.' I inhaled deeply in one swift moment, stabbing the needle straight through.

IT WORKED! Holy crap it actually worked.

See, this is where I fucked up. The needle was stuck... I couldn't pull it out... for 12 hours... yup... 12 whole hours.

Love for Xu Wu

John Truong

———

It's been nearly a year since I've talked to Xu. I've noticed that since he's been staying home, he's probably working as a YouTuber or Twitch Streamer making money by playing games. I've also noticed that Timmy has been obsessed with Xu as well, to the point where during the Year 10 yearly exams, Timmy stalked Xu by hanging around outside his house for a few hours. This obsession was not healthy, as we think this might as well be showing Timmy's love for Xu. Even our Maths Teacher, Ms Khodary, has pointed out that between Xu staying home all the time and Timmy stalking Xu, Timmy can't keep up in class.

Now, the only thing we can do is wait for Xu Wu's return, as his return will bring us happiness and most importantly, the opportunity for us to tie him up and keep him in school.

Timmy is still distraught over the fact that whenever he confesses his love to Lidiya, she always turns him down.

In Chemistry, we were meant to be doing our work when in fact, we had a talk at the back of the class with a classmate. Our classmate Maroun was a psychiatrist, therapist and a counsellor for another classmate, a girl who has been giving people strange looks. Her name would not be revealed due to privacy. She was also another person who could call Timmy weird, which built up the negative affect on Timmy to the point where he would also need to seek help. Whilst we were chatting, she suddenly got aggressive and went too far by saying she didn't like to see Maroun's face. Maroun was surprised by this and turned to me.

'Am I nice?' he asked me.

I replied, 'Yeah bro.'

Maroun knocked the girl's textbook down, which gave Timmy an opportunity to help her by picking the book up and handing it back to her. This was Maroun's magic of giving Timmy therapy whilst giving the girl therapy as well. Timmy, who was mentally broken as this point, slowly reached down and the weight of the negativity he had kept inside him dragged him towards the Earth, causing him to lay down on the ground. He tearfully grabbed and lifted up the book, and turned to the direction of the girl. He said whilst stuttering, 'Here you go.'

He fell down and started throwing a fit. His cries were continuously annoying as he was pouring out his emotions. I didn't know what to do in this situation. I mean you don't see a 16-year-old having a fucking fit every day. 'Don't worry m8, it's not your fault,' I told him. 'There's always Xu,' I joked.

'Yeah, you're right, I can stalk Xu,' Timmy replied while wiping his tears.

'Yeah, you could do that.'

Western Sydney

Michel Anderson

—

Foot after foot, I skim the perimeters of Sir Joseph Banks High School. Arms swing in harmony, caressing the soft breeze emitting a familiar scent that is unique, demonstrating it belongs to this grand school. Above me is the bright blue curtains that overlaps the sky whilst the bright yellow spot is radiating colour to brighten my day. My love for this school is boundless due to the nature such as trees and grass that dresses the school fields.

I never enjoyed the city as much as advertised by society. To my left, to my right, above me and below is hard, plain concrete with little to no greens. Such an emotionless world enclosed by the nature of finance and business. Distant from the true beauty of our world. Maybe this is why I respect the Indigenous people of Australia so much, as their ideology is to preserve the land that houses them. I can firmly claim without an ounce of doubt that this school is the greatest. A school in which cares for the keepsake of nature far exceeding the beauty of any other piece of land in Western Sydney. The principal, the teachers and students despite being different whether it is through beliefs, race, culture or the elixir that runs through our veins, all share our love and care for the physical environment of Sir Joseph Banks High School.

Iman

Marouf Alameddine

—

To the men and women who fasted today:
Surround the barbecue,
buy the ka'ak and cheese craved all day.

One-third food, one-third water, one-third air.
This was the Sunnah of our Prophet Muhamad (PBUH).

The thought of food makes us salivate.
But it isn't the food that brings us joy at the day's end,
rather our connection with a Being so divine.

Allows us to clear our mind
and repent for being so blind
to the sins we committed...

Never could a month be so Great and Beloved to Muslims.
Men make their way to the masjid in their abayahs.
As do women, wearing their scarfs.

We pray.
Pray we live to see another month of Ramadan –
the month that replenishes the iman of all practicing Muslims.

Guard Up

Ebony Annor

—

Brown, thick and loose curls sit on Wali's head. Wali is sitting on the park bench outside of the Morris Iemma Sports Centre, head in his hands. He looks up at me. Black eyes turning brown in the sunlight. He's wearing his black AUSA Hoops jersey and his grey and orange basketball shorts. 'Oh hey Ebony,' Wali says.

'Hi!' I say, surprised I managed to speak. 'Are you ok?' I ask him.

'Yh I'm fine.'

'Ok well, I gotta go train. You coming inside?'

'Na.' I turn and start to walk towards the sliding doors of the building. 'Actually, yh I'll come.' I look in the reflection of the glass doors as Wali gets up and walks over to me.

When he reaches me I look at him and he flashes a smile, but it doesn't reach his eyes. I don't say anything though. We walk in silence and when we get to the court he goes over to the boys and I go to where Coach is training a few kids. I want to have handles like Kyrie. After training was finished we stayed around for a while shooting and playing 1v1s.

After playing against my brother I was exhausted and decided to shoot around when I heard someone say, 'Guard up.' Now in basketball terms this just means, let's play 1v1, I start, you defend.

I turn as Wali puts the ball in my hands. I check it to him. And he dribbles straight past me and lays it up. Playing against a cocky future basketball legend sure is fun. But the next time I checked it to him I didn't let him pass me that easily, or maybe he just wanted to show off how good he was with the ball. Either way I reckon I was defending him pretty well, totally not fouling him as I pushed and played aggressively. I mean it is street ball. Every time I tried to block his hook I could feel the strength in his arms and when I pushed him or touched him I could feel his muscles underneath the fabric of his shirt, and it was kinda hot. There's this tension between us like it wasn't just a basketball game but hey maybe that's just me. Eventually we had to go home ya know so I guess that all ended.

A few days later landed in New York ready to start his NBA career. So yh I really liked this kid and he just got up and left. Yh... don't ever love anyone with skin that isn't yours.

bà

Jessica Vu

———

Tam ran into the direction of the plump and rounded figure that stood at the outer edge of the kitchen sink. The smell of her phó lingered around her and had gone tugging at the hungry nose, which then jerked the rest of her body into the kitchen room. Her bà immediately let go of the chopstick she had been rinsing. Wiping her teary eyes with a stroke of her index finger, bà embraced Tam running to her for an affectionate and yet long-lasting hug that she had been yearning for at least three long years. Tam boasted in delight and squeezed her grandmother's chest with excitement. When they had finally let go of each other, bà planted blessings on both of the Tam's chubby, round cheeks until she had complained of how fat they were. Tam had one last look at the pot resting on the table, and tugged at her grandma's warm hands.

—

Tam loved staying with her grandma in Vietnam. Her parents would travel back to Bankstown to continue working after spending half of the holiday with her. Tam loved her chubby and cuddly bà. She would trade all her teddy bears just to see her. Her grandma had decorated Tam's room with puffy cushions, a thick mattress and a group of cuddly bears. Grandma had chosen the book of the newly bought pile of favourable Vietnamese ancient stories. Tam's homesickness instantly disappeared as she saw the groups of teddy bears, and with warmth she laid on the soft bed that her grandma had tucked her into soothingly. Tam smiled as she saw her grandmother open the book that she had chosen. Tam was fond of her bà nôi's storytelling, as it had put her to sleep.

—

Tam releases the rectangular plastic sleeve out of her hand and onto the table. Taking the blue pen out of the sleeve, Tam writes her name using printout letters on the HSC booklet. It is the HSC finals. Tam is nervous but her hands make their way to the jade pendant for comfort. It is the pendant that her bà had given to her, and the thread she has used to create the necklace that she wears. It is the last item that her grandmother had given to her, and Tam knows how happy her bà would be.

'If only she was here.' Tam quickly blinks away at her watery eyes, and looks at the clock on the wall.

—

Tam sees the bus she needs to get to Bankstown Hoyts before her friends would start watching the movie without her. Running to the bus stop stand, her heart is pumping out of her chest. Tam's breathing is getting heavier and heavier at each interval. Gravity like her body weight is pulling her down, making it seem impossible to catch that bus. She doesn't like running, but she needs it now. The bus leaves without her. Tam is late. Too late. Tam thinks of running after that bus but she knows that she won't make it. Just like her HSC, she has five minutes left. Those five minutes left are her chance to finish answering the last question that will prove to the rest of the world that she has finished on time. Tam couldn't find the answer to it, and time had always made her late.

—

'What do you guys want to be?' asks Anika with the emphasis on the Indian accent.

Anika with her wavy long dark brown hair looks at Tam, wanting an answer. Tam has heard this question many times, and when she hears it she senses her dead grandmother. A loss of Vietnam, and a loss of heritage, the loss of homemade phó and the loss of Vietnamese stories. She misses her bà. Six years ago, Tam's parents had told her that her grandmother was in the hospital fighting against cancer and that they promised her that the family would go back to Vietnam to see her. Tam was eleven and when they got to the hospital, had been told that she had passed away a week ago. They were late. They knew Tam's bà had suffered. When thinking about it, Tam wishes she was with her bà while she was going through pain. Tam wishes she was beside her, reading her stories and making her phó.

Tam looks at Anika, 'I want to be a doctor.'

They smile at her, nudging each other and whispering to each other. 'Did your parents force you?' Chen asks.

'No,' replies Tam. She knew that they would ask that.

Kalitsounia

Joanne Georgousaki

—

When I think of my grandma, the first picture that comes to mind is her kitchen. Old white cupboards that have turned yellow over time. Smooth tiled floors in old-style fake marble. Fridge covered in Greek postcards and photographs stuck with magnets. One wall covered in pencil mark to show how tall I've grown. I can finally reach the tap and open the freezer after all this time.

My grandma and I spent a lot of time in that kitchen. She is the one that taught me how to knead dough and pass it through the machine and into thin sheets ready to be filled with cheese and spinach to make kalitsounia. Fold the pastry over like licking an envelope. Brush egg and sprinkle sesame seeds. I always got excited when we baked. Every Easter and Christmas my grandma would make koulourakia to celebrate. She was strict with tradition.

She taught me that I need to Lent during The Holy Week and she would take me to church for Holy Communion.

My grandma was the person who first showed me around Bankstown. During the summer holidays she would wake me up to go to the local markets and buy fresh vegetables and fruit. After the shopping she would sometimes buy me sugared donuts for being good. Go home. Have compulsory afternoon naps. Wake up before dinner. Cut fruits and eat them from cups and look out the window together.

Punchbowl

Jaafar Ibrahim

—

I was chilling with Hadi and his older brother Ali who were my neighbours at around 11pm. We had just finished a feed at Punchbowl KFC. It was a Saturday night and we were playing basketball in the front yard. As we were playing, a loud bang came from a car driving by. It was an old shitty Corolla. We ran to the side of the road to see what had happened when the car stopped and rapidly turned around, heading straight towards us. It was some White dude and his girlfriend aged around their fifties. As they pulled up into our driveway, we sprinted back into my house, afraid that they may have a weapon. Minutes later there was a knock on the door. Afraid to wake my parents up I opened the door slowly to the man in the car standing there with spit around his mouth.

'Where are your parents?!' he yelled in Bogan. My mum came to the door and he yelled straight at her, 'Your fucking kids threw a rock at my car. Nearly had me a bloody accident!'

After about five minutes of complaining that me and Hadi hit his car, he went to show us the damage. Bogan showed me the dent on his bonnet and I bursted out laughing, 'Bro, that's just rust!'

After ten minutes of denial Bogan said, 'Oh wait, that's an old dent. This is where the rock hit.'

Still laughing I looked at the new spot, 'Bro, that's just texta mark!'

Bogan denied it again and went to lick off the mark with just his tongue. When he licked it the mark went.

Laughing until I felt like I had mad abs I said, 'Is there anything else you want to show us we did? Maybe a cigarette burn?'

Swearing his head off about getting the cops on us, Bogan got into his car and drove off. The cops never came.

Fingerguns

Amanda Yeo

—

I know I'm screwed pretty much straight away, but the way I know I'm the extra special kind of boned is when she turns to the guy pouring cement next to her and says, 'You should ask if she has any concrete plans this weekend.' Then she cackles, he rolls his eyes, and I fall in deep infatuation.

She's still laughing as I cross my driveway to the chain-link fence that surrounds the construction site. Some Inner West couple are turning next door into a duplex. No one who lives in Panania can afford a place here anymore. She has a messy brown ponytail, wide nose and Sailor Moon shoulder tattoo, and she's leaning against a pile of bricks like she's selling knockoff watches in an alley.

'Hot out, isn't it?' Woah, slow down, you master of conversation, you wizard of observation, you star.

'Huh?' She turns and looks at me, and I did not think this through. My entire face is heating up. I'm ninety per cent sure I'm glowing like a traffic light.

'It's getting hot out here.' Because my brain hates me it launches into the chorus of Nelly's 2002 classic 'Hot In Herre', so I miss the beginning of her response. I miss the end of her response because she is still looking at me and I remember that I am still wearing my pyjamas because I wasn't planning on leaving the house today. I don't know if these are the ones with the hole in the armpit. I keep my arms at my side, just in case.

'I'm Lian.'

'Sue.'

'Oh! Like–' and here I stop because the only 'Sue' I can think of is 'A Boy Named Sue', but I've started this sentence already so I finish it with 'Suuu... san?' Only I say it like I'm falling down a well or like I'm her dead father coming back in the clouds to remind her of who she is.

'Nah, just Sue. Like, "I'll sue you".'

Was that a warning? Am I annoying her?

'Sorry about the noise – we'll try to keep it down.'

'Oh no, it's fine. I just – I was wondering if you'd like a drink? Since it's so hot. Thought you might be thirsty.' I should just go back into the house. Regroup. Form a plan of action. Maybe die of shame.

She shoves her protective goggles on top of her forehead. It pushes the flyaway hair back from her eyes, intensifying my feeling of being appraised. 'Ah, nah, I'm good. Thanks.'

'Well, if you need anything, you can ring my bell. I'm home all day. Marking essays. Family law. Which is funny because under the law I can't have a family!' I fingerguns at her. Oh my god, I fingergun her. And now it's super obvious I'm hitting on her, 'cause what kind of moon unit volunteers that information unless they're trying to get up on you?

'I should get back to it.'

'Nice to meet you.'

I doubt it was that nice.

—

I can't leave the house now. She's there all the time, laying bricks, cutting wood, measuring things. I can see her from my kitchen window while I eat breakfast. I just know that if I go outside she's going to look at me again, and it's going to be awful.

I don't even need to go out, really. I could survive just ordering everything online. I don't trust other people to pick out my vegetables, but could put up with it until construction's done. I know I'm being a coward but I'm allowed to be a coward in my own home.

I'm looking over lesson plans a few days later when the doorbell rings. I swing the door open, and Sue is on my front porch, sleeves rolled up and brown eyes on me. She has the most toned forearms. 'Hey. Do you have any duct tape? You said I could come 'round if I needed something.'

I am living in a hell of my own design.

—

The best way to conquer your fears is to face them head on, so the next time we speak it is on my terms. I've showered, I've combed my hair, I've put on actual human clothes without holes in the armpits. Nice clothes even, this white floral dress that I probably should have saved for a date, but I need to get a date first. I've put on make-up so it won't be obvious if my head spontaneously combusts, and I've spent a minute doing power poses. Sue's by the fence, sitting on a pile of wood and drinking from a thermos. I still can't read her. She wears flannel, but that's like the tradies' unofficial uniform. 'I was going to offer you a drink again, but it looks like you've already got one.'

'Yeah. Coffee.'

'Cool. I prefer tea.'

She nods and offers a polite smile. I get a glimpse of a crooked tooth before she takes another gulp from her thermos. I should have practiced hitting on people in high school. This is like if my first shot at dancing was as the lead in *Swan Lake*. Fortunately, I have prepared a list of topics of conversation. Number one is her job. You don't see that many women in construction – or at least I haven't seen that many. If she doesn't want to talk about that, number two is the weather. Cliché, but it has been very hot lately, and depending upon her response I can pivot it to climate change, which most people have opinions about. Number three is cats. Everybody likes cats. But before I can begin, she swallows and asks, 'Where are you going?'

'What?'

She gestures vaguely at me, and I look down at myself. Oh right. I am going somewhere because dressing up to stand in your driveway and talk to the construction worker next door is weird. And I am a super normal person. 'I have... a teaching training day.'

'Ah, so the master becomes the student.' She says it a little weird, like those kids in primary school who used to fold their hands and bow at me. I can't tell if it was intentional or not, but she looks Islander so I give her the benefit of the doubt and laugh. 'Something like that, yeah.'

'Don't let me hold you up.'

I don't have my keys, so I have to pretend I've forgotten them and go back into the house. Then I come back out and drive away, even though *Judge Judy* is starting in twenty minutes, because it'll be weird if I don't come out again. I circle the neighbourhood for a while, burn some petrol I can't afford, then head to Macca's. I order two Big Macs and I eat them both.

—

This is stupid. I am a fully-grown woman. I'm not going to be held hostage in my own home. I am going to go outside, I am going to exchange pleasantries, and I am not going to run away and eat half my daily kilojoule intake in one sitting. This is what I say to myself whenever I look out the kitchen window for the next week.

—

I'm on the treadmill trying to burn off those Big Macs, all sweaty and out of breath and too exhausted to think clearly, and I've had enough. No woman is worth this amount of exercise. I stumble off the machine, stagger my jelly legs over to the front door, and throw it open before I lose my nerve. Sue is smearing mortar on top of a half-finished wall of bricks. There's a couple of men in fluoro polos doing something with wood a few metres away, and I have a wet bib of sweat on my shirt.

'Hey!' Sue looks up as I approach the fence. My heart is beating out of my chest and my knees are wobbly but I lock them in place.

I have to do it now. Just do it. Do it. 'Do you want to get a drink?' Sweat drips down my forehead, stinging my eyes, and my mouth is a desert.

'Nah, I'm good, thanks. Still got some coffee.' She turns back to her bricks, scooping up another trowel of mortar and plopping it on the wall. Breathe.

'No, sorry, I don't mean now. I mean at a pub or something. Later. If you want. We could go. You and me?' She looks at me again, brow slightly furrowed. My leggings are riding up my butt.

'I don't drink.'

'Oh.' Something in my chest unravels, and my eyes start to water. What did I expect? I don't want her to see me, but she'll notice if I try to hide my face. I need to leave. 'Okay, never mind then. Thanks.' I turn away.

'I can do coffee.'

Wait, what? I look back and Sue's hooking her fingers in the chain-link fence on either side of her head. 'Or tea. You like tea, right?'

'Right. Yeah. Tea. Let's do tea.'

Sue breaks into a wide grin. Her crooked front tooth peeks out. 'Right. Let's tea it up.' And then she fingerguns me.

Gold Digger

Suleiman Suleiman

—

A wise man once said: *She don't believe in shooting stars but she believe in shoes and cars.*

Well even if he is a bit retarded these days us boys dress just like him.

'Have you heard? Yeezy is at Culture Kings!' shouted Abu Hashish.

'Yei cuz I fucking get it!' yelled Ali.

Abu Hashish was more excited than a Wog in a kebab store. This was his dream to meet the Notorious Kanye West to give him the biggest roast of his life. 'Yallah ya sick cunt let's go to Punchbowl Station.' Abu Hashish jumped into his favourite Nike trackies and Adidas hoodie.

'Reckon Kim is with him cuz?' Ali asked. 'I heard fake ass feels like wet cement.' Ever since Ali watched J.Cole's *No Role Modelz* live performance, where he made that fat ass statement, he has wanted to chuck a *Myth Busters* and suss it out himself as he used to be a bricklayer.

'There's one way to find out cuz, just be patient,' said Abu.

Abu and Ali made their way to Punchbowl Station. They didn't even bother to use their Opals. Bloody Wogs. They made it to St James and when they saw one of the inspectors they gapped it no joke. George St was damn hell filled with hypebeast twelvies with fake Yeezy's and HBA hoodies and of course, the tourists who don't even know who the fuck Kanye is let alone pronounce his name right. The boys ran into Culture Kings. They even stole some Aussie kids' snapback. There was Kanye motherfucking West and his missus Kim.

Ali put the Skip's hat over his crotch, 'Nah cuz, her ass is natural.'

Abu was about to piss his pants laughing so he started roasting Yeezy, 'Cuz you made a song called "Gold Digger" but you married the girl who doesn't believe in shooting stars only fucking shoes and cars!'

Culture Kings went full crazy and Abu and Ali gapped it again screaming, 'YEAH THE FUCKING BOYS!'

On the Way to Sydney

Omar Sakr

—

Yellow fields ask too many questions for the sky
to answer. It refuses to lower itself

to what is knowable, a local geography
of facts. Occasionally it will rain

a torrent of dream, a world of water,
more than we need or the field requires.

I can't keep any of it in. My hair gleams.
I am a child again spilling free in Lurnea,

an Arab boy among others, a boyhood of colours
locust mouths descending on the mall,

heavy with need. Heavier with regret. Or
desire. One thing we never lacked

were questions were bruises. No copper
no security no mother could stump us—I

remember, I wasn't at the scene of the crime
that's not even my name, this isn't my house

or my country, I'm telling you I'm not even here
right now, I am somewhere else writing a poem.

It's okay. I have what they call a photogenic memory.
It only retains beauty. Or else what it holds

is made beautiful given enough time.
Like my grandfather feasting on a snake's head

to survive in war-worn Lebanon. Like boys
in Coles stuffing pockets with stolen answers.

923 Bus

Cloe Letele

As the wind blew through my long curly hair I waited for my 923 bus. Ten minutes late again. Tick tick tick tick. With every second I started to panic more and more. Sweat started to flow down my forehead. I began to picture the disappointed, frustrated look on my teacher's face when I walk into class late. Great, just what I needed, to get another detention, all because my bus was late.

Four more minutes.

I look down to see small ants crawl across the cracked concrete below my feet. I notice they are carrying little crumbs with their delicate legs. My bus is fifteen minutes late as it appears around the corner. I tap my Opal card onto the machine... Bing! A whole seventeen minutes late.

A Hijabi's Fitted Dress

Bassima Hadid

—

'*I3ama ba3yoonik lesh festonic dayie 3alayki hek, hala* watch what your dad is going to do to you *wallah ley khazoo*,' Mum yells when she sees me walking out of my room wearing a black lace fitted dress.

I start clenching my jaw while looking at myself in the mirror. Hearing keys unlocking the front door, I read *Ayatul Kursi*, blow in my hands and wipe over my whole body. The loud, hollow footsteps begin echoing in the corridor on the shiny white tiles. I feel my heartbeat get slower then faster now getting the gut feeling that I most definitely will not be walking out of this house wearing this fitted dress.

'Hi Baba.' I swallow looking up, his thick dark eyebrows turn into a mono-brow and his eyes widen.

'*Wleh hek tal3a men albayt, roohi enebri shlahi*, rissspect your scarf!'

With no reply I turn around in absolute silence, feeling nothing but anger fill my body, silently asking myself why *hazi khara*? 'I don't know what to wear!' making my voice echo through the house.

Before I know it Mum comes storming into my room, '*Wleh* all that you have in your cupboard and all that I buy you and still have nothing to wear. *Hala* I'll show you what "I don't have anything to wear" is.' She pulls out half my cupboard and chucks it onto my bed. 'Bassima, I am going to give you ten minutes, if you're not finished by then *wallah* I'm leaving without you.'

I wish that clothes just randomly appear on my body. I begin to throw them all around my room like a *kawtha*. Brown shirt, green top, purple dress, all flying around in the air.

'What do I wear?' Tears running down my face, my mascara smudging and snot dripping from my nose. Finally an outfit catches my eye, a gold lace top, baggy black skirt and a cream scarf. Throwing them on as fast as I can and not giving a shit about how I look, I walk out of my room meeting face to face with my mum.

'Just in time, *shefti* now *jesmik meno embayan* and you are *emsatra, yallah* let's go and *inshallah* I will find you *3arees* and *Allah bi rayahni menik*.' (Just in time, see now your body isn't showing and you are modest. Yallah let's go and inshallah I find you a husband and God relieves me from you).

Wallah

Eman Arja

—

'*Ya abu badr!*' This tall Sudanese sweaty bearded man yelled on top of my head. I squeezed through the crowd of different raced men and hijabis that were filling up the street of Lakemba. Lakemba at night was crazy. There were groups of about ten Arab men in each café smoking their hubbly bubbly. There was so much traffic, cars beeping and drivers yelling at each other.

At night-time Lakemba had no parking, people parked anywhere there was a free space that fit their car. There were little shops that were set up everywhere that were selling many things like hijabs, sahlab, kaak, corn on the BBQ and burgers. I turned my head and looked around. There was this fat old lady in a pink niqab sitting on a milk crate on the side of the road feeding a baby in her arms. She reminded me of a sheep. I think I'm going to call her Em Kharoof, which means Mother Sheep. I looked away from Em Kharoof and tried to catch up to my family. I was with my Aunty Laila, my cousin Fouad, their three children Adnan, Bilal and Maya and my sister Ibtisam. There was a group of Egyptian men walking towards me. They looked like a herd of camels. They were stubborn, they spat a lot, they had curly hair and were smart asses and carefree. A group of Arab men were sitting in a café. They were chewing like cows with their mouths open, food going everywhere and yelling at the top of their lungs. We walked past all these stands that were selling food and clothes. It smelt like sweat. There were people everywhere shouting and yelling at the top of their lungs to each other. We walked to the stand where a short skinny guy who looked like a meerkat stood.

'You want *batata* on a stick?' My cousin Fouad looked up and told him to make us seven. He paid the man and we just stood waiting. I watched as he put the potato into a machine and tuned it till it looked like a slinky. He then put some batter on it and put it in the deep fryer. We all picked out what salt we wanted on it. He sprinkled salt and vinegar flavouring on mine and handed it to me. It was a crispy texture and tasted very salty. I turned and looked at my two-year-old cousin Maya in front of me.

She poked a lanky lady in a purple hijab and green dress in front of us until the lady turned around and yelled, '*Ya Allah bseb emek wallah abooki!*

I looked up at the lady in disgust. Bro, what idiot yells at a two-year-old? I grabbed Maya and held her the rest of the way. I was beginning to get claustrophobic from everyone so I asked my Aunty Laila if we can go into a café. We went into a quiet café on the corner of the street and sat down. I told Fouad what happened with that *hmara* lanky lady and, as Arabs do, he started yelling.

'Why didn't you tell the lady off *wallah* if anyone talks like that *la binti, wala bint 3ami, ha kaser ros jidon*.' He banged on the table and glared at the floor.

'It's funny what Ramadan can do to people's temper,' I said.

'It's the lack of *dekhan*,' my aunty replied.

Lakemba/Punchbowl

Farah Abdelkarim

—

/ *Lakemba Mosque*

At Bankstown on Thursday is like *Eid-ul-Fitr* at Lakemba Mosque, but in this situation the only thing different is there are lots of sluts and fuckboys roaming around in Centro. Girls like Mari to Hussy and boys like Ali dw to Musy from the corner shop, all bunched up in groups with the cigar hitting their crusty ass lips as they laugh like a bunch of hooligans thinking they're cool yet they're all undeveloped, all coming to Bankstown not to buy anything, just to kickback and smoke some hashish. As Majnoon and Kalb walked in the slidey door shit in Bankstown, Shayma's eyes poked out like a hawk and she choked on her kebab. As she was walking past them, her shoulders collided with Majnoon and Kalb. As their shoulders touched, Majnoon's shoulder hit Shayma's shoulder so hard that her kebab went flying in the air like a Jetstar plane.

Shayma screamed out, 'Bruh, what is this ya ugly *putas sharmootas*,' hands crunched up together in a form which was so close to Majnoon's face.

Ali dw and all the Laylas crowded around ready to watch this 1 on 1, shouting 'throw and fist!' but instead Shayma kneeled down, grabbed her kebab off the dusty floors of Bankstown and took a piece of the dry kebab and wiped all of Majnoon's make-up off with just that piece of kebab.

Then as Shayma was wiping Majnoon's face she said, '*Shu hal araf za el zarame, wallah roohy mooty ya* Bankstown *sharmoota*.' And as the crowd started ooing and shouting 'What a savage!' Shayma walked off and realised that Majnoon was a trans.

/ Ramadan at George's Chicken

Walking in a normal pace trying to keep up with my maturity.

Entering the shop that was filled with tables and chairs and people. Some from Bali and some from Tonga, speaking, laughing and choking on their chicken bones with their spit roaming the air.

As I ignored and walked past them, the smell of chicken hit the atmosphere and rebounded into my nostrils, it made me crave some chicken bone. I scrunched up my nose, remembering I had to wait for Maghreb, that was in another 20mins so I distanced myself before I got out of my way and felt the chicken hit my lips. As I was waiting the clock was going tick tock tick tock then all out of the blue I heard a huge BANG! I ran as quickly as I heard the sound. I saw a distraught girl who had dark chocolate hair tied back and an apron which had stains. The smell of this girl got me blocking my nose and holding my breath in, it got me thinking she had never had a shower. Then I heard this deep loud male voice from the back of George's Chicken screaming, 'Really Aqueela, do you want to lose your job today, aye?'

As he said that water started oozing out of this girl Aqueela's eyes. I didn't know what to do so I grabbed one of the pans that had fallen on the ground, then adjusted my positon facing her head, then I went 1, 2, 3, swung the pan back and forth, then BAM! She fell face on the floor. I bet she had a concussion but I just said bye habibi and left.

Malay

Evelyn Araluen

—

malay cracks the morning
and pries suburban from the scrub
the first time I've heard her in this hazy place
where lawns edge bush brushes
and tyres swing from goanna trees
where blue eyed babes won't
walk beyond the fence line
cos those dodge city boys
might be looking for a feed

she don't follow me through town
when I speak her that way
this cobblestone mountain shadow town
rivering up settlement grants
and decaying into city spread

dad's not worried
like those other honeyeaters
got him worried
reckons they're here to push out the rest
to soak up all the green sprouting
from that last big burn
  that one
  when he refused
  to leave

I swear it wasn't like this before
never heard that snap or bell drop
never had to pay for the M4
where I saw nothing but tree on that horizon
a scene of semi-rural whinge

I went back the other day
  to dodge city
council must have fixed up the dam
but it's still that same dust
those same boys bumming smokes
bruising bellies on crumbling bike mounds
crashlining crucifixes from londonderry to llandilo

after I could go to woollies
after I could swing by COSTCO
after I could see a doctor or catch a train to town
get that city commute down to fortyfive by twentytwenty
drag the city to dodge
  and bring back maccas on the way

I drive to castlereagh to remember my horizons
maybe wear my feathers to remember emu scrub
I leave the path in yellomundee
and try to sink deep enough
       that I become skin amongst skins
       that has no other memory of this place

just before dusk
I collect two minutes thirty seconds
of an old gahr filled gum on my phone
to watch again and again
as their white wings slip gold in sinking sun
as their song rattles still enough sky

I show dad
as he washes up after tea
we watch as we are mountain watched
       remember this call
       remember enough

Harambe

Farah Abdelkarim and Shayma Assaad

—

'Farah *roohy jebili koosa min* Lakemba *ya hmara*,' hollered Farah's mum at her daughter while her and her friend Shayma were laughing at Billy's mohawk on Instagram.

As they ran to the car before Farah's mum swore anymore, they saw the neighbour and he was screaming, 'Happy Ramadan HO HO HO,' but they were in a quick rush so they couldn't say anything back.

As Farah's mum booted them outta the car with her elephant-sized foot she screamed, '*Bedi el kosa a3dar min hashesh wa edek* ten minutes *bedi 3mal el akel.*'

As they were walking down past Abu Omar's butchery they saw Harambe's twin but with bigger feet. Farah stopped and looked at Shayma saying, 'Isn't Harambe dead?' Then they both started laughing like dying chihuahuas and realised it was Suzie, their best mate from school.

As Suzie's ape shoulders collided with theirs, they stopped and spotted and spoke for a while. They were too busy thinking about the boost, they didn't care to listen to anything she said but the only thing that slipped through their ears was that she was fasting. As they got the *koosa* and were walking back to the car, Farah's mum caught a glimpse of them and started running behind them with her *shahata*. They chucked the *betenjan* that they mistook for *koosa* on the floor and ran as fast as their legs could carry them, stopped because they were out of breath, huffing and puffing. They stopped and ate pizza at Pizzaland, only to see Suzie the fat cow munching on some pizza crust. They ran towards her and they both pulled two huge *kafs* on both sides of her cheeks and then they ran back to Farah's mum. Back to IGA to get *koosa* this time.

Weo Weo Weo

Norita Rizvi

———

I ran after my sister, she had already crossed the road. I hadn't even gotten halfway through when something hit me. It happened so fast I didn't know what it was.

Roaring... roaring of the brakes of the continuous beeping. The sound slowly fading as the only colour I could see now was black.

Weo weo weo is what I wake up to.

Mum is not there... MUM IS NOT THERE.

I try to get up but I can't move. Tears raining out of my eyes, it feels as if needles are being stabbed into my body. 'Please stay calm and tell me your name, you're going to be alright,' says a paramedic. That was the last thing before my blurry vision turned into black again.

Myuran Sukumaran: Part 1

Shirley Le

—

We're sitting in the science classroom writing letters for Amnesty International. At the end of the day, we'll post them to Singapore to protest the death sentence of an Australian on drug trafficking charges, Nguyen Tuong Van. The Bunsen burners at each desk give off a gassy, charred smell like singed rubber. It makes me feel paranoid, like something is burning in the distance but no one can see the flames or hear the sizzling. '*To whom it may concern, the death penalty is cruel. Please give Van another chance.*' I stuff the letter into the front pocket of my school bag.

That afternoon, I catch the train home on the Bankstown line. I lean against the door, feel the wind brushing the back of my legs as it blows through the grates. The only other person in the carriage is an elderly man who is flipping through his copy of the *Sydney Morning Herald* with Frankfurt fingers. I squint and read the front page, the headline for the day is: 'Police want death for Bali Nine'. Photos of the nine young Australians are captured in a grid and their names are printed underneath each portrait. Renae Lawrence and Matthew Norman's photos show them smiling into the camera like the friendly young people on my learner driver's booklet. Myuran Sukumaran's photo is positioned in the bottom row, next to Renae. The photographer has captured him looking over his shoulder. His eyes are in mid-blink. He looks confused and half asleep. The train lurches forward and we're slowing down at Canterbury Station. A group of girls from Canterbury Girls High get on like a band of sewer rats and they eye my brown uniform. There are five of them, three Fobs and two Lebs. They wear their blue uniforms with white Rabens. One has her school shirt unbuttoned all the way. Underneath it is a yellow basketball jersey that has 'Cook Islands' printed on it in a thick cursive font. Her frizzy black hair is pulled back in French braids that snake along her scalp. The hem of her school skirt grazes against knees thick with purple scabs and one of her Rabens has a phone number written on it in pink highlighter. No one at Sydney Girls is allowed to customise their uniform like that.

'Oi, what are you starin' at? Who said you could stand in my spot?'

I tense and look away. Cook Islands moves closer to me. I catch a whiff of a familiar rose scent and realise that we use the same deodorant – Impulse Illusions. I bought mine from the Bankstown Woolies for two bucks one night. According to Impulse, Illusions is the perfect scent for vivacious girls with boundless energy. I want to tell Cook Islands that I'm not trying to start anything, I was just admiring the way she wore her uniform. But before I can explain, she pushes me against the door of the train. My arms shoot out in automatic defense. We grip each other's shoulders in a deadlock. Her arms are strong with shiny black hairs sprouting from each pore. Mine are half the size with bones popping at the wrist. Cook Islands' nostrils flare out like a bull. Her purple lips curl inwards against her teeth. Her Fob and Leb friends are shrieking and drumming their palms on the seats. 'Get her Christine, mark your territory!' I clench my jaw and push back, lifting my spine off the door. Christine seems to give way but she's smirking as if she knows something that I don't.

'Next stop, Campsie.'

The announcement catches me unaware and I loosen my grip. Christine seizes the opportunity and shoves me extra hard so that the back of my head slams against the door. A dull ache spreads from that area like a cobweb. I place a hand on it, expecting to feel a dent. Instead my flesh is tender and throbbing beneath my fingertips.

Christine smacks her gum and shuffles off the train with the other girls. The soles of their Rabens scrape along the floor and there's that smell of burning rubber, only this time, it goes away as soon as the doors shut. The old man is also gone but his copy of the *Herald* is left behind. The front page with the Bali Nine has been ripped in half and the piece with Myuran Sukumaran's face has fallen to the floor. The paper is crumpled. The light from the setting sun is shining through the west side of the train. It's partially blocked by the graffiti and grime smeared across the window. Myuran Sukumaran's face is doused in a slate grey and he has a thick five o'clock shadow. He keeps looking over his shoulder as if he's waiting for someone behind him. I fumble through my bag and check if the letter I wrote in the morning is still there. My fingers touch the edge of the envelope. I hope I get to the post office in time.

—

'Let's hear some news from Geoff the Gay Newsreader, get on with it Geoff!'

Kyle's voice crackles as my friend Trung swerves the Mazda from the left lane into the right lane. We overtake a white Toyota utility loaded with construction materials. We pass the Yagoona Salvos where people dump old clothes everywhere in front of the store and cockroaches swarm all over them, the KFC where school kids have contests to see who can eat the most chips, the TAB where old anxious Viets smoke and the hot pink Mr Cheap store that has packs of toilet paper in the front for a dollar. Geoff the Gay Newsreader reads through his news bulletin: 'On Wednesday, Andrew Chan and Myuran Sukumaran were transferred from Kero-boe-kayn Prison to Nusae-kam-ban-gain Island, where they are expected to be executed by firing squad.'

Trung shakes his head and whistles through his teeth. He squints his thick black eyelashes together, turns to me and says: 'Those two guys went to my school – they were just unlucky. Drugs are quick money, that's all it is.' Trung flicks to Bankstown 100.9 FM. Tupac's deep and clear voice blasts from the speakers with a piano melody in the background: *'Instead of war on poverty, they got a war on drugs so the police can bother me.'*

Trung drives with his right hand on the steering wheel and his left hand on the gears. I don't know why he needs to do that, the car's an automatic. The sleeves of his white school shirt are rolled up to his forearms. He's always been so tanned that when I first saw him at Yagoona Station, I thought maybe he was Malaysian since they're closer to the equator than us Viets. Trung's maroon school tie is half undone and flaps against the wind. He's chucked his Year 12 jersey in the passenger seat. It's got 'FTP' printed in big black letters on the back. Once, I asked him what it stood for and he said 'Fuck The Police' but then he told the principal that FTP were the initials of his grandfather from Saigon: 'Phó Đặc Biệt'. That actually means beef noodle soup with different cuts of meat like tendons and stomach lining.

We pull up at a set of lights and Trung's eyes dart sideways at the bright yellow sports car in the right lane. 'Check out the tats on that guy,' Trung says to me, cocking his head at the car.

I can't see the guy's face but I can see the blue inked scales of a koi fish snaking down the elbow that's sticking out of the driver's window. There are light blond hairs all over the pale freckled skin making the koi fish look furry. The punk rock music coming out of the car makes its way into my ear, head and heart and my pulse beats in time with it. A male voice warbles and whines to the screeches of an electric guitar: *'Sometimes I cannot take this place, sometimes it's my life I can't taste.'*

I watch the arm sticking out of the yellow car, its fingers are a splotchy red. Stubby with square nails cut close to the skin. When the light flashes green Trung slams his sneaker down on the accelerator and the rest of the Hume tries to catch up with us.

Myuran Sukumaran: Part 2

Stephen Pham

—

Birds blip from the park with no name next to Cabramatta Creek. I'm sitting in my backyard under a custard apple tree, flipping through the *Sydney Morning Herald*. One headline reads, 'Hundreds farewell Sukumaran at Sydney funeral'. In the article Myuran Sukumaran's sister remembers watching *The Babysitters Club* with him. She says that he enjoyed it, even though it was a TV show for girls.

Over the fence, the thud of a bunted ball announces the start of a footy game. I wonder what a young Sukumaran, who was raised in Western Sydney, would have seen in a show set in fictional Stoneybrook, Connecticut, where even the houses were white.

I never watched the show, but I read a couple of the books at Cabramatta Library. I spent a lot of time there when I was ten years old and Mum was going to TAFE. We were too poor for a babysitter, so every day at 4pm, after she closed up her computer shop, she walked me through the streets of Cabramatta.

I kept my eyes on the ground, scanning over the orange plastic caps and dark splotches of gum, spit and blood on the concrete. I pointed at needles half silver half black and Mum kicked them into the nearest drain, saying under her breath, 'Si khe ma thuy.'

We walked through the sliding glass doors, past the front counter made of smooth, cool stone in a horseshoe shape, and into the kids' section, where the colourful letters of the alphabet pasted all around the room made the grey tables, carpet and walls seem greyer. Then Mum left. There were other kids, sometimes playing with their friends, sometimes screaming while getting dragged out by their parents, sometimes just colouring at the desks. I never talked to them. I stalked up and down shelves, scanning spines and pulling out books at random.

One time I pulled out a *Babysitters Club* book. The title was spelt out in cubes like alphabet blocks for kids. There was a picture of two girls, one with black hair in a bob, arms crossed in front of her body, and circular glasses taking up half her face, glaring at the girl to her right, who had a side ponytail and loose black and orange jumper, mouth open and striking a pose with arms angled out like she was doing a dance. In front of them a little boy with the red hair and rosy cheeks of Alfred E. Neuman stuck his fingers in his ears. It looked boring and gay, but I read it anyway.

By the time Mum picked me up, I was the only kid left in the room. I put the book back on the shelf. We went past the counter, through the sliding glass doors, and past an ambulance up on the curb. Paramedics were trying to resuscitate a man convulsing on the ground. The man wore a loose black T-shirt. I'm pretty sure it had Bugs Bunny and Taz in the centre.

I suddenly hear a high-pitched scream shoot out over my fence, followed by deep, choppy chanting. I realise it's the haka. The Pasifikas must be playing football at the park again. I fold the newspaper and put it next to me. I take out my phone and search for The Babysitters Club on YouTube. There are two episodes. I watch the one called, 'Claudia and the Mystery of the Secret Passage'.

A scene opens with a Georgian house, two storeys painted white with blue window shutters. The camera zooms into a window then fades into the interior. Claudia is bent over, dark hair hanging thick and straight, the only Asian girl in the room. She's looking at a piece of paper held by a girl wearing a detective hat. 'It's probably been in the secret passage for over a hundred years,' Claudia says in a squeaking voice. 'Or even longer,' says Dawn, who has long blonde hair and is standing on the far right. 'Our house was built in the 1700s.'

Over the fence, the war cry from the Fobs continues, screams dipping and rising in pitch, with a couple bursts of 'BWEH'. I look up into the branches, where baby custard apples hang heart-shaped, green and bumpy.

I'm wondering why I read so many *Babysitters Club* books. Maybe Sukumaran and I both liked *The Babysitters Club* because it had nothing to do with us.

—

I go with high school friends to Bar Century for $3 shots. Both levels of the bar smell like mouldy shoes. Next I head up the road to ZAIA. Entry is $20. I hand $25 to a fat brown guy with a stubby nose like a gargoyle for a cap of MD. The club is filled with smoke, green and pink lasers cutting through, bodies in billowing Tarocash shirts and cling-wrap dresses convulsing to doof-doof music. I'm dancing holding a drink when I feel a clap on my back. I turn around. It's the fat brown guy, gargoyle nose studded with sweat. He hands me a cap which I swallow without looking. My body feels light, like it is dissolving into the music, and wherever I go—from the sweaty dance floor to the bar backlit in gold to the ventilated smoking room—I dance.

I get back to Cabramatta Station at 6am.

The walk home takes twenty minutes, navy sky overhead, road to my side silver under the amber streetlights, everything so still and silent I turn around every couple steps in case someone's following me. The landlord's dog, a black Great Dane cross, barks at me. I go into my house, which is the landlord's garage. I shower and pass out.

When I wake up I smell the damp stink of booze and cigarettes. I open the window. The night sky's purple. In the combination TV room and kitchen, Mum's at the stove, her back to me. Beef and green beans are sizzling and spitting, and the sharp smell of soy sauce rises with the smoke. The TV's on, showing an Anglo-Australian walking around a prison that has grey walls, turquoise bars, and some purple flowers poking out from green leaves in the corner of the screen.

Mum asks me if I opened my bedroom window. '*Muoi ru thuoi quac*,' she says. 'You reek of booze.' I pull my shirt out at the neck, sniff, and say, 'Yes.'

Myuran Sukumaran is on the screen. He blinks hard and says: 'You see all these people like in night clubs with nice BMWs, and nice Mercedes and there's always chicks there, and they was buying drinks for everyone and you think, *Fuck, how do you do this on a mailroom salary?*'

The sizzling in the kitchen eases and Mum is standing in front of me, one hand on her hip, the other holding a spatula. 'See?' she says, pointing the spatula at the screen. 'All your friends want to trick you. Only family is there for you in the end.'

καλιιερα

Mariam Al Asaad

My mum and I walked into the tall pointy black gate. The first thing I noticed was a sign saying, '*Αγίου Ιωάννί Δίμοτικό Σχολείο*,' meaning, 'Saint Ioannis Primary School.'

Above the sign there was a white flag with a yellow map of Cyprus. My heart was beating really fast and I was shaking. I squeezed my mum's hand.

'*Shu*?' Mama asked. As we entered the building a tall, fat lady with brown eyes, brown hair and tanned skin was waiting for us.

'*καλιιερα*, Mrs Carmel and Mariam — it means good morning,' she said softly.

'*Alhamdoula*,' I whispered to myself, 'Finally I know what that *καλιιερα* means.' It had been buzzing in my head from how much

I heard it on the street. The lady's name was too difficult, so I decided to name her Big Fat Mrs Brown. Big Fat Mrs Brown led us to her office. Her desk was very neat and clean with gold writing on the front saying, 'Principal's Desk.' Her chair was black leather and it felt so comfortable.

Big Fat Mrs Brown pulled out a pink folder with my name written in cursive with a blue pen. 'Could you please check if the information in the folder is correct?' Mama nodded. She looked through the pages in the pink folder one by one.

'It is all fine,' Mama said gently.

'*Εχαρειστο*,' Big Fat Mrs Brown said. 'Mariam can start tomorrow.'

Oreo

Hikmah Tebe

—

Safiah and I sit on the couch watching TV as black and white Oreo, almost two months pregnant, walks in. Her pace is slower and her large belly is prominent. She wanders around in search of a spot to spend the next few hours. She is startled, I take a step back as her first child emerges into the world. The room has flipped, Safiah has her hands in her hair mumbling words as she paces. I grab a pile of old clothes turning to see Oreo running onto the balcony. A black and white ball in a clear sac hangs, swinging side to side out of Oreo as she runs frantically in circles. I place the old clothes down, putting on rubber gloves.

'Safiah, get the tissue box!' I walk out and sit down as Oreo has slowed her pace. I gently pull Tofu out. Sofia hands me the tissue box and phone.

'Zhara is on the phone!' I place my phone on my shoulder, tilting my head to hold it down as Zhara helps me through what to do. I feed Oreo the placenta.

Ten minutes later she breathes heavily. Tempeh passes through. Again I wipe the kitten and feed Oreo the placenta. I gather the clothes around Oreo like a crater. Huddled warmly near Oreo another four pop out in the duration of six hours.

Sik Chik

Tamar Chnorhokian

—

The hallway of the tech centre was crowded. I navigated my way through a sea of mauve coloured shirts and wide-pleated black skirts until I reached Gusia's side. '*Inch bess ess?* How are you?' I sung out.

Gusia turned her head sideways, her eyes as round and dark as a blue moon. When she spotted me standing there her eyelids dropped and she smiled as sweetly as a Disney Princess. '*Luv em. Toun inch bess ess?*'

'Hungry.'

Gusia reached inside her locker and grabbed her books and gold plated lunchbox, which reminded me of my mother's woggy jewellery box. It was carved with bird and flower patterns. We turned the corner and walked down the white lino-covered hallway with grey concrete walls until we got to a double-glass door which led to the courtyard. Girls were scattered everywhere sitting on the asphalt ground, some sitting on the metallic benches underneath the eucalyptus trees. The buzz of conversation was so loud it was like we were two fans at an Ed Sheeran concert trying to make our way to our seats before the show began.

'Your bro's a jerk,' Layla yelled from under the trees. Her nasally voice always made my head hurt.

'Hey skank, let's take a selfie,' Cindy hollered like a crazy rockstar – she thought she was Pink.

Nayiri was sitting under the metal awning of the textiles building. It had been our hang-out since Year 7. It was a good spot providing the right amount of shade and sun and it was close to the canteen and the toilets. I knew Nayiri through the Armenian community. When we were younger we saw each other occasionally at parties. As soon as we started at Smithfield Girls High School we realised we were the only two Armos in our year so we stuck to each other like The Kardashians. In the first week of Year 7 our PE teacher, Mrs Sanders got us to create a dance routine as an icebreaker. She paired Nayiri and me up. The two of us put together our Armenian dancing with some Indian Bollywood moves to 'Love Story' by Taylor Swift. The dance was so fun that Mrs Sanders made all of Year 7 do it as a warm-up for the rest of the term. From that moment on all our classmates called Nayiri and me Little Skits.

Nayiri was leaning against the brick building with her eyes closed and headphones plugged into her ears. Her Cornetto-shaped legs stretched out and her short skirt lifted all the way up to the top of her thighs. She had sprayed her ivory skin with coconut oil. The smell was so intoxicating I wanted to eat her for lunch. Her school diary was lying open beside her and the top line of her last entry said: *Zayn Malik is the hottest guy ever.*

Gusia and I stood there for about fifteen seconds watching her. Nayiri's eyes were still closed and she had begun singing the words to Dua Lipa's hit – shaking her head from side to side, ash bob hair flicking her high cheek bones. 'I could be the one, be the one, be the one.' She belted the lyrics like she was a contestant on *The Voice.*

Finally, I swung my right leg back and playfully kicked her with my black Skechers. 'Hey shithead, wake up.' She flinched and her head hit the brick wall, skirt flying up revealing her white undies.

'Ouch!' Nayiri's eyes popped open. '*Mayret!*' She looked down at her bare legs and quickly pulled down her skirt.

'Your mum,' I replied, poking out my tongue.

Suddenly there were screams coming from the middle of the courtyard, the words 'bitch' and 'slut' and 'backstabber' blasting through the air. The voices sounded as shrill and crude as the women in the WWE. I sprinted towards the ruckus and pushed my way through the crowd to find two girls circling each other. One was Nadia. The other was Claire. They were both in my math class. Twenty or so other girls on the playground that day gathered, standing anxiously, wondering what was going to happen next.

All at once Nadia stomped her stumpy thighs on the asphalt and clenched her fists tight like she was about to do the haka. 'He's mine, you *gahba* hoe!' she spat as she got up into Claire's freckly face. 'Not anymore you fat bitch,' Claire roared back. Her white face was turning pink and she began to look like strawberry shortcake.

'What did you call me?' Nadia lunged at Claire's head and began yanking her ginger ponytail with her Michelin hands. She was tugging so hard that Claire became a cawing crow. Claire tried to break free by scratching at Nadia's hands with her coffin nail acrylics but it looked like she was only scraping the surface of Nadia's bulky arms.

The crowd of girls had grown larger now and there were random jeers being thrown around. 'Smash that meat pie!' Nadia's Assyrian friends shouted. 'Flatten that kebab!' Claire's Aussie friends retorted.

Finally, I jumped into the cat-fight, wedging myself between the pie and the kebab, trying to push them both as far back as possible. Not being around boys made the girls extra territorial and fights like this broke out all the time. Sometimes it was for major reasons like stealing one's boyfriend and other times a girl could just be paranoid and jealous and start a rumour which lead to a three-second brawl. 'Stop it you psychos!' I yelled as I tried to pull their hands apart. Nadia's grip was so tight that I couldn't make her budge and all the while I was being clawed at by Claire's sharp nails, pins poking into my flesh.

In all the chaos I could hear Nayiri yelling for me, 'You tell em, Arevig.' This time I tightened my grip around Nadia's chubby wrist and shoved it hard. Her hand flew high in the air and for a moment it looked as though she was praying. At the same time, Claire lost her balance and fell to the floor. Nadia was about to pounce again but I stood in front of her with my arms crossed.

'Where are you going?' I asked, cocking my head to the side.

'Arevig! Stay out of this!' Nadia said, looking past me at Claire, who was stumbling back up to her feet. I noticed that her skirt was dusty and she had a few scratches on the back of her left arm. *Boy, that girl was frail!*

Suddenly, a deep familiar voice boomed, 'You three, come here now!' We turned around to find Mrs Petrovic emerging from the cluster of girls. She stood there shaking her head, thin lips pursed tight.

'Miss, I was trying to break it up, I swear.'

'Yeah Miss, she was,' Nayiri said as she came forward, followed by Gusia who stood sheepishly beside her. Mrs Petrovic gave me her nod of approval. Then she walked away with Nadia and Claire in tow, who were both giving each other death stares. The rest of the girls dispersed, including Nayiri. That's when I realised there was something up with Gusia. She was standing in the middle of the courtyard, where the girls had just punched-on, frazzled like she had been blasted in the face with a hair dryer...

Pitbull and Maria

Shayma Assaad, Farah Abdelkarim
and Aqeela Shauab

———

As Maria was tryna look sexy walking in the streets of Punchbowl past George's Chicken, Pitbull from YouTube started whistling like a *jahash* outta his cheap ass Toyota Camry 2000 model with the turbo burning every time he drove a meter. Maria blushed as Pitbull winked his Fetty Wap eyes in her direction.

'Meet Me at the Hotel Room,' started playing and the bass popped off.

Maria was in a hurry to catch the train to Al Aseel to have *iftar* with Sally from down the Punchbowl alley. Pitbull parked that cheap car of his in a bus zone; all that was on his mind was Maria and getting her number. Misguided by her long brown hair, big brown eyes and her slim hourglass figure, he jumped outta his car and adjusted his Nike hat in a suitable position. He followed Maria up the flight of stairs to the train station. Without getting a train ticket, he jumped on the train Maria was already in. He saw her sitting so he chose to sit two seats directly in front of her wanting to speak to her. Behind her he saw the boys in blue checking passengers' tickets.

'*Yel3an hazi*' – god hates my timing – he whispered to himself. As he waited to get off the train at Bankstown he ran all the way back to Punchbowl where his cheap ass car was parked and realised it was towed.

Bigge Park

Catherine Prasad

———

Last card, na you cheated, no, yes, I can see five other cards underneath your fat thigh. Can we change the game, we've been playing this for like four hours now? I'm hungry. Shotgun for the aux cable. Chris you driving. Well I'm the only one with a licence here. I vote Catherine to pay. Guys I didn't get paid this week. Why? I talked back to my boss. OMG way to go bumface. Wasn't my fault, she spits when she talks and her monobrow looks like a caterpillar ready to transform into a gigantic mother butterfly. Catherine you need to respect your boss even if she has a monobrow. Yeah I will when she learns to talk without spitting. Guys I'm hungry. Ayeee I saw this poster about free food at Bigge Park. Well let's go, if it's free food everyone's going to be there. Hey where's Catherine? If I know my girlfriend she's probably running already. We look outside. You guys stand there and talk, I'm going. She isn't even wearing shoes. That's my baby. Well let's go. We get there and all we see is a bunch of people. Dark, white, fat, hijabi. Damn this line. Guys follow me and do as I say. Bubba on the count of three fight with me. Baby you want me to punch you? No you idiot, like verbally. Oh I thought I get to punch you. You wanted to punch me, how dare you? Well sorry you're a bitch. Asshole like you're even better? At least I don't post pics for other guys to see. At least I don't check out girls' asses when I'm with my girlfriend. OMG that was one time. You mean one thousand times. Baby you're over exaggerating. While we're fighting and distracting the people, Ryan spots a trolley and takes all the food and grabs us and tells us to run. We bolt it back and get into the elevator. That was the fastest I've ever run and all for free food. Worth it tho. Guys we forgot to get drinks. OMG JESUS. Baby if you want to go outside and be attacked by hungry animals be my guest. Nah I need my hands for something else today. You guys disgust me. Netflix anyone?

Sharia and Cigarettes

Peter Polites

—

/ *Dallas*

Few years back I knew a guy who called himself Dallas. I met him when I was sitting in a café in the middle of Bankstown Plaza. I was drinking a long black and writing in my notebook. I'd just had a terrible breakup and was listing reasons why I didn't need a man, all of which I got from women's self-help books:

1) Lean in to love... yourself.

2) Only you can be the best you.

3) The universe has your back: Transform your fear into faith.

When Dallas walked past, I noticed the way his khaki shorts fell just below his knees. Wore a thin polo shirt that showed off milkshake smooth skin. He walked past once and looked at me. He walked past again in the other direction and our eyes met. Suddenly he took the pen out of my hand and wrote his name and mobile phone number beneath my list on the notepad.

I called him in the afternoon and he was in my bedroom by the end of the night. He appeared in my doorway wearing imitation G-Star jeans that had diagonal stitching, he carried a Gucci satchel and wore leather sandals.

In a thick woggy accent, he told me that he was French. I asked him to speak French so he did. He said, *'Jemapelle Dall-ass du pa la, ha hub A-La bonjor.'* Sounded like gibberish.

We had sex in my bedroom that night. It was mechanical. He removed his clothing instead of waiting to be undressed. He was circumcised. All the Europeans I've slept with have foreskins. That was my second clue. I said to him, 'I think you're from the Middle East.'

After sex, I suggested we go out for a meal, but Dallas refused to be seen in public with me. The next day he came over, shut all the blinds in my apartment before we sat down.

I had seen it before. The Freshies – fresh off the boat, smelling of saltwater, their hyperactive eyes filled with anxiety, tightness in their shoulders.

The gay boys from overseas, always afraid. Back in their homeland, Cousin Ali whispers to Sheikh Mohammad who talks to a cop. 'I saw him with a man.' Concrete and metal bars and the tic tock tic tock time is ticking until the sting of a sword on the back of your neck.

/ Lion

As I turn onto the Hume I nearly run over a teen on a hoverboard. He is wearing Nautica shorts and a Tommy Hilfiger T-shirt. He eats a manoush slowly, concentrating on each bite, putting more and more into his mouth. Stuffs more of the bread between his thick lips as he balances on the board.

I put my foot on the brake, my neck whips from the sudden stop. My car two feet away from him. He keeps his eyes on his food and continues rolling.

Get a park right in front of Sultan's, the manoush bakery in Yagoona. No relief from the sun as I walk in. Wall of heat. Behind the counter the old hijabi is molding a wad of dough. She stops and looks me up and down. I order a zatar with vegetables. Her eyes squint and a smile expands across her face. She calls out, 'Fahad... Fahad... Come and serve this handsome young man.' I am confused. She's usually the one that takes my orders. She winks at me and then continues to dig her hands through the dough.

Out from the back of the restaurant a man in his thirties appears. He has hairless limbs and big bovine eyes. The cuffs of his clothes are dotted with flour. His eyes expand, almost bulging out of his head. 'Hello! You want zaatar broda?' I nod, give him my money and tell him I will be waiting outside.

Over at the rival manoush bakery across the road, people come out, holding the thin bread. Four Lexus jeeps and a flock of motorbikes go by, mufflers grunting. A woman in her twenties walks past me. She wears a leopard print scarf over her head, an ankle length black cotton dress and a pair of Versace vintage sunglasses. She glares at me – one of those what-the-fuck-is-this-dickhead-looking-at looks.

'OMG. I totally wanted to buy those Versace Aviators on Eyegoodies but they sold out.' I do a gay gasp to give context clues. 'I love that Versace are doing a throwback to the nineties.'

'Fash is totes cyclical,' she says. 'Like I mean those Nike Jordan's are back.' She points to my shoes, then skips off down the street. A valley girl in a burka.

A while later Fahad walks out with my zaatar. His shorts fall past his knee, thighs press up against fabric, calf muscles protruding like rocks in a mountain. His tight lips expand across his face. He gently places the wrapped manoush in front of me.

Fahad lights a cigarette and sits opposite me. I lift the manoush to my mouth, unsheathe the white paper off the bread and then I put the whole roll as deep into my mouth as possible. The bread is warm and soft, just the right amount of oil connects the thyme, oregano and roasted sesame seed.

'You know my name is Lion?'

'I know Fahad is a common Saudi name,' I say to him.

'You very smart.' He smiles, taps his head with his index finger.

'Not really. I Googled it.' I wink at him. He opens his mouth and exhales the desert winds in a laugh. I see his teeth. Straight little squares. All in perfect position. A middle class smile at odds with his broken English. I ask him for a cigarette and reach out my hand. He opens his packet and delicately places one in the middle of my palm. We both hold one another's gaze, a bunch of Leb men in full garb walk past. '*Manouks*,' they say. 'Pooftas.'

Before Fahad comes over to my apartment, which is on the other side of Yagoona, I tidy up. I pick up my dirty clothing from all over the floor and shove it into my wardrobe. I collect empty Coke and VB cans which are sitting on the coffee table and the kitchen benchtop and throw them into my recycling bin. Arab boys grow up in houses where their mothers follow them around and wipe their arses. They hate mess.

When he knocks on my door I'm looking for condoms. He stands in my apartment corridor in the clothes he wore to work today. The hems of his jeans dusted with flour. Oil stains on the front of his T-shirt. He smells of greasy body musk, pungent herbs and Lynx Persian Rug.

I make him a Turkish coffee. We sit on my balcony and look over the Bankstown train line. 'So did you come to Australia for love?' I ask.

'No,' he answers. 'If I stay...' He places his hand on my knee. His index finger curls up and down my thigh. I put my hand on the back of his neck, run my pinky along the line where the hair meets the skin, where the sword would have made its incision.

White Converse

Safa El-Mazloum

—

I walked into the mosque with my mum, little brother, sister and three cousins in front of me. We were in the downstairs empty car park due to the other women's section being full. I could smell feet, and then I noticed that I was near the shoe stand. There were brown closed shoes to red and blue shoes that were embroidered with small beads. I placed my white Converse on the stand that was amongst the brown shoes. I sat down next to my mum while my sister took care of my brother. The carpet was bluish-grey and rough, the walls were white, in a corner there was a big screen that showed the sheikh standing. His beard came a little past his neck and was grey with specks of white. He was wearing circular glasses and a white cap on his head. I looked behind me and saw a wave of women sitting all bunched up.

The sheikh started the adan for Isha, '*Allahu Akbar, Allahu Akbar.*' When he finished we all stood up raising our hands close to our ears and placing them on our chest to start the prayer. When we finished we all sat down while the sheikh gave a lecture.

All of a sudden I heard my brother yelling, 'Muhammed Salallah.'

I turned around to see my brother sitting in my sister's lap with a big smile on his face. I turned around to face the front with my head down. The sheikh talked about how technology has made us lazy and how most people don't do things with sincerity, they do things because they have to. When the sheikh finished it was time for Taraweeh. I had to change my spot due to filling in the spaces. The sheikh started so we all followed. I went down in sujud. There was a woman's feet in front of me. She was wearing aqua socks with a patch of dirt at the heel and toes. I dodged her feet by putting my head a little to the right. The sheikh finished so I put my head to the right then put my head to the left seeing a woman's head still to the right. We all stood up again ready to pray Witr. On the last rikah we cupped our hands catching our dua.

In unison everyone said, '*Ameen*' and '*Ya Allah.*'

Orange

Tien Tran

—

Hieu, the dickhead, wins $43,822.00 from Division 2 Oz Lotto, and the first thing he does is he goes to the Subaru dealer on the corner of Walter and Beaufort and buys a bright orange WRX. He texts me, *im gunna doit*, then an hour and two minutes later pulls up to my parents' driveway in a juice coloured rice burner that looks like a video game. The spoiler sits so high that you can see the tip of it from the front. I think to myself, *Oh my god, what a piece of shit*. The engine switches off and shakes itself to a halt, like that shake your body can't help doing at the end of a piss. The grills on the front bumper and bonnet look like smiling black teeth. Hieu comes out of the Rex, a haircut that splits his hair down the middle of his head and frames his forehead with a McDonald's M, the same haircut that every Viet in high school had, including myself. If fifteen-year-old me saw Hieu now, riding through Northbridge in his stupid-ass orange car, the extended fringes of his middle part flapping in the wind like tentacles, I would've called him Big Bro in front of my friends. Hieu shakes my hand, grinning. 'What's with the hair, kunt. You tryna be a spiderboi?' I ask him. He runs his left hand through the side of his left fringe. 'Don't be jealousss.'

Everyone calls Hieu 'Đen', which means black, because he's a dark-skinned Viet. He's big for a Viet too, tall and broad shouldered, but he has a hunchback from years of being bullied and folded in half by his older brothers. I met Hieu in uni but I knew of him in high school. Our postcodes belonged to different districts so I went to Mt Lawley and he went to Mirrabooka. Mirrabooka had more Viets because they had the Girraween, Balga and Westminster kids. Mt Lawley had more Chinese, Serbs, Croats and Bosnians because it was a fob school for ESL'ers.

We do a small tour around the Rex, the sun beams off the orange paint and makes it painful to look at without squinting. Ants crawl along the exposed aggregates of the driveway and into the shade under the tyres. The wheels are so new that they still have the protruding rubber hairs and the smell of cured chemicals. The odour makes me light-headed. We walk around back of the car. Hieu puts his hand on the spoiler, patting it as if it was his kid's bottom. Then he leans against the car with his shoulders tilted, his chin jutting around as he talks while his hands slap each other. I put my arm on Hieu's shoulder, 'This is the dumbest thing you could've done with your money.' His eyes dart around. 'You wanna get some bubble tea or what?'

Back in our uni days, Hieu and I never went to any lectures because we couldn't wake up early enough. Curtin had just introduced e-Lectures, where they filmed every lecture and you could watch it on the portal. My home internet sucked and Hieu didn't even have internet, so we'd come in at the end of the week, usually 3pm on a Friday, and catch up on that week's lectures in the Engineering computer lab. Hieu would pick me up in his all white 85 Commodore. It was an old police car that his dad bought at an auction. Curtin University was south of the river, all the universities were south of the river except for Edith Cowan, which everyone called Super-Tafe because it had low entrance requirements. The drive took us thirty-five minutes, which is a long time in Perth. Usually we had the whole lab to ourselves, row by row of tables with the exact same monitor, keyboard, mouse and computer chair, but sometimes the international students came in to watch Asian drama shows or the Arabs studying Chem Eng were already there playing *Counter-Strike*. I liked to sit in the last row with the light turned off for the back section of the lab, relying on the light of my monitor and the front of the room. Hieu said it was because I wanted to look at porn. He sat in one of the middle rows but on the opposite side. It took about six hours to cram in the week's worth of lectures about geotechnical soil testing, yield strength of steel reinforced concrete and shear stress in pre-stressed concrete. Civil engineering is pretty much about guessing how much force we can put on concrete, steel and soil before it breaks, snaps or collapses.

One evening, two Hongkies in Jordan 3s with the tongue pulled out of its laces so that it looked like a Nike billboard for their feet, were smoking on the footbridge out front of the lab as we left. A brick path extended from the bridge and wrapped around the courtyard. At night, the light poles made the pavement look orange and cleaner than how it looked on our way in, without the cracks and scrape marks. The sharp twang of electric guitars and thuds of drum kicks from The Tavern echoed across the empty courtyard. The Tavern was an old brick building that stood out of place amongst the newer structures with curved concrete walls and metal pillars. The wooden doors and floors were water stained and smelt musty and acidic, as if the odour of beer and vomit were soaked into the timber. We sat inside at a table with a bowl of crinkle cut chips and sour cream and sweet chilli sauce, and a bottle of Corona each. A tall wiry White guy in a white singlet, pink boardies, donning a green afro wig, who knew all the words to 'Mr. Brightside', swooped past our table and picked up a chip from our bowl. 'Yeow!' he screeched, singlet latched to his bony torso exposing his sharp shoulder blades, which looked like the corners of a table. I had an urge to yank his puka shell necklace from behind and clothesline him. Hieu watched Mr. Brightside walk around the pool table to his four friends who were all wearing something stupid, one of them in that lime green Borat mankini. Borat wrapped an arm around Mr. Brightside's shoulders and smirked his fake moustache as he talked. 'These cunts have never been bashed before, have they?' Hieu said loudly above the music. Mr. Brightside glanced at us briefly. Borat kept the smirk but his eyebrows fell flat. I wondered if I'd ever get used to the familiarity that White people have with strangers and if maybe us Viets were too uptight and worried too much about saving face all the time. 'Fuck those cunts.' Hieu sipped from his Corona, thumb and index finger wrapped around the bottleneck. We both forgot what we were talking about before and decided to leave as the whole bar started clapping along to the tambourine intro to 'Are You Gonna Be My Girl'. The car ride home, I watched the trees pop out of the dark and into the high beams of Hieu's 85 Commodore as we did 120 down Tonkin Highway. In the side mirror, the trees fell back into the dark. I let out a 'yeow' to break the silence. 'Fuck kunt, don't even start,' Hieu said. We spent the rest of the trip talking about how funny it would've been to fight a guy in a green afro and a Borat mankini.

My arms stick to the leather seat of the WRX as the 2:32pm sun aligns with Tonkin Highway southbound and roasts us. I look at Hieu. 'You gonna turn on the air-con or what?' Hieu winds the windows down but the hot wind burns our faces so he winds them back up straight away. I ask him why the hell he doesn't just turn the air conditioner on. Hieu snaps at me: 'Cos I gotta feed this bitch 98 octane. It's like a dollar forty-five a litre.'

Shu?!

Aya Elgamal

—

The smell of *mloukhiye* and *mansaf* fills the room. Mama is calling me to help her in the kitchen. I run in and she hands me the hot plates of شوربة عدس, *shoorbat addas*, to place on the table. I put them on the table without dropping them. Fatma fills a plate with *tamar* that we got from Coles. Ding Dong!

'Oh shit, they came! Fatma go open the door.'

'I'm fixing my hair,' I say.

My sister gives me a death stare and tells me to open the door right now. I have no option but to open. Holding the doorknob breathing in and out I get my face ready for sloppy kisses. I open the door but it is Baba.

'*Ezeyek ya benti?*' How are you daughter? he said in his Egyptian tongue.

'*Alhamudilah.*' I'm good. Please tell me they didn't come. 'Oh *ya Allah* they're here,' I say quietly. I know they are Lebanese from their fair skin. I've never seen these people in my life.

'Oi Fatma,' one of the ladies tells me. '*Yi kifik* Aya, *eshtatelek kteer.*' Oh Aya I missed you so much. She gives me four sloppy kisses on my right cheek. Her fluoro pink lipstick stains my face. She kisses me like she is kissing a cow.

'Sorry *ana ma barefek, ma sheftek bi hayati.*' Sorry I don't know you, I've never seen you in my life.

'*Ana bar arefek*! I know you from when you were a beebi,' she says.

My mum greets the guests and invites them over to the table. '*Yala hay aden el mughraib*, come on it's nearly *aden el mughraib.*'

'Mama who are these people?' I whisper.

'They are my mum's sister's brother's aunty's children,' she says.

Shu?! What?!

Conversations: feathers, quandongs and tracks

Emma Hicks

—

To me artmaking is a conversation – I do not understand creativity as a solitary consciousness or act. My art practice is about finding a way to offer a space for others to move within. Conversation is a powerful tool but it is not only words... it is also behaviours and actions.

When I was generously asked by Michael Mohammed Ahmad and Winnie Dunn to provide six artworks for this anthology, I was thinking about reciprocity. How we are affected by, and in turn affect, other bodies in both historic and idiosyncratic ways? There is a relational ethic to this, carrying with it responsibility for the spaces and the places which we inhabit.

In a conversation, what is not said is often just as important as what is. The six ink drawings that I have provided in these pages represent moments that have shaped forms of recent conversation, but they resist time as a linear concept – they cross between times, punctuating different times. There is an old tree in my front lawn, memories are etched onto its surface, it structures feelings – relationships ebb and flow around it. I take the hair from my hairbrush and place it under the tree and the birds come to use it for their nests. A brush turkey leaves me a feather on my front door mat. My brother stops by to give me some quandong seeds he has collected. The lorikeets come in the afternoons. A crow swoops. An echidna comes to the fence.

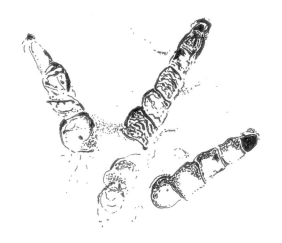

Brush turkeys

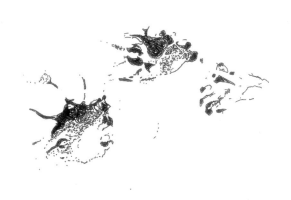

echidna

Lorikeet

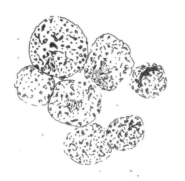

quandong seeds.

Second Plate

Samar El-Charif

—

My eyes moved to the big ticking clock that sat in the far corner of my spacious lounge room. I realised it was only 3pm. I groaned loudly and fell back onto the couch, my throat drier than the Sahara desert.

'Mum, I'm hungry!' I called out in a whiny voice. My mum was in the kitchen, wearing a cheap apron whilst she fought to cook what seemed like three hundred different meals.

'Just sit down, *adan* will be soon!' she called back, daring me to speak again.

I sighed and moved my eyes to the TV once more, watching the food channel as my stomach growled. It seemed like food was everywhere around me today, just teasing me, the knowledge that I couldn't put anything into my mouth until the sunset. As I broke out of a sudden daydream, my younger sister made the wrong choice and decided to sit next to me, munching on my favourite chocolate.

'Here have some, Samar, I won't tell Mum,' she said in a whisper, a sly smile plastered on her innocent face. She knew what she was doing.

'Go away!' I screamed and shoved my face in a pillow.

Ramadan was always a hard month for me, I was a food-lover and didn't like to be deprived of it. With my head still in the pillow, my breathing calmed down and my eyes closed as I fell into a heavy slumber. I was sitting around the dining table, varieties of food laying before me, cups filled to the top with chilled water. I was just about to take a drink when my eyes flashed open, my dad towering over me trying to get me to wake up.

'*Yallah* get up, it's time to eat,' his deep voice echoed. As soon as I heard the word 'eat' I shot up, now fully awake. The sound of the *adan* ran through my ears prompting me to start running to the dining table. When I got there, my other family members were already sitting at the table. I forgot that they were coming over to break their fast this evening.

I grumbled hello and picked up my glass of water, bringing it to my lips. The water quenched my scratchy throat. Greedily, I sat on the table and put everything onto my plate, my mum telling me to slow down but I played deaf. It felt strange to have food in my mouth, almost unnatural, but it was short-lived as hunger took over. When I managed to look up, I saw my family laughing and chatting. It was then I remembered why I loved Ramadan, it brought families together without a fight. I smiled to myself and put a second plate.

Sister Sister

Abigail Chand

—

'Sister, sister.' That's what she says when she tries to sit in our car. On a cold, windy afternoon my ma is yelling at me saying, '*jaldee karo*,' which means hurry up in Hindi. I am getting the groceries out of our white 4-wheel drive and my ma is standing behind me with her hands full with grey plastic bags that contain fruits, vegetables, chips and lollies such as strawberries, blueberries, tomatoes, celery, salt and vinegar chips and Starburst lollies.

Just about when I was going to close the car door, my ma and I hear someone behind us saying, 'Sister, sister.'

We both turn around to see a middle-aged Lebanese woman who is wearing a dark green hijab, a pink shirt with the word 'swag' peering through, white baggy jeans and a green handbag to match her hijab.

Again, she says, 'Sister, sister.'

My mum says in a serious tone, 'Is everything okay, do you need help?'

She repeatedly says, 'Sister, sister' before walking up to my ma and patting my ma's back. I'm staring blankly, asking myself, *What the hell is going on?* The lady just stands there in silence for a few seconds, then walks up to me, stares at me for a few seconds, then proceeds to walk a few meters to the car and sits in the back right passenger seat. My ma races to the car after putting the groceries down on the ground. She asks the lady politely if she can get out of the car. The lady responds by waving her finger in the air to say no.

After a few seconds go past the lady asks my ma if she can drop her to Bankstown Macca's so the lady can eat a Big Mac. My ma repeatedly asks her to get out of the car. After a few seconds of the lady staring at my ma, she then proceeds to get out of the car saying, 'You're no fun!' in a whiny tone and then walks away as if nothing has happened.

Jumper

Monikka Eliah

———

My nana knitted rows and rows of black and white Vs. She huddled me into her bedroom where the other grandchildren wouldn't see. She tried to shut the door but it bounced back from the frame, held open by a plastic bag full of fabric that had been hung over the top corner. Standing between Nana's single bed and the wooden bedside table, I stared at a plastic statue of the Virgin Mary. The only coloured sections were her pink toned face and the edge of her blue veil. The dark pupils of the statue had been mistakenly stamped just left of the indentations marked for the eyes. I imagined my grandmother at night holding the length of her cotton nightgown in her hand, baring her chicken sausage legs, thick and pale and covered with purple and green veins, her grip dampening the fabric with sweat as she struggled to bend down onto her swollen knees to thank the statue. Nana's face would tighten as she pulled herself up to stand and begged for her father, '*Oye babi, Oye babi,*' to lessen the pain.

My nana let out a grunting sigh as she stretched her fleshy arm up to the top shelf of the cupboard. I watched the wrinkles smooth out as she reached up, her thick fingers fumbling for the familiar texture of what she had hidden. She smiled as she snatched at something that made a rustling sound. Then she gestured for me to come closer. Her hands were quick untying the knots. A bag in a bag in a bag and then a jumper. It was wide enough to fit two torsos and the sleeves stopped just short of my wrists. Nana had decorated the chest with white wool knitted into a triangle that stopped just above my *shartha*. I couldn't remember how to say I love you, so instead I told her, 'It's so hot,' and hugged her. Her warm body smelt like *koobah* and sweat. The wavy hairs sticking out of her bun tickled my neck. When she pulled away she told me not to kiss her face. '*La nashketla pathee, soh-ten.*' By contrast my '*La-ah*' seeped out slow and messy like tea from the bottom of a cracked mug. I put the jumper back into the plastic bags, tucked them under my T-shirt and walked into the hallway weaving through my younger cousins. They were lying down with their bare bellies pressed against the kitchen tiles. Inside the kitchen was my Aunt Suzy, who was always left to clean up, her long white arms elbows deep in soapy water.

I didn't wear the jumper until almost a year later: sitting in the lounge room eating soggy avocado toast with lemon juice and watching *Millionaire Matchmaker.* I started to feel a little cold and ran to my room. After sniffing the sour tinge of sweat dried into the armpit fibres of three different jumpers, I found the one Nana had made. I pulled it over my head quickly. The wool scratched at my face. Then I walked back to the living room in time to see Tony the car-selling millionaire complaining that Debbie didn't let him 'have her cookie' on the first date.

The jumper was thick and stiff. I tried to stretch down the sleeves to cover my wrists but the wool wouldn't shift. I ran my hands along my chest, smoothing down the places where the fabric had buckled, until I noticed a silver thread poking out of the centre of the white triangle. I tried tucking it back into the Vs. A loop of it bounced out a little further down the line. It was thin and the texture varied from straight to wavy. I tugged on the end and as the thread pulled out from my chest I realised it was a long strand of human hair. It was my grandmother's, knitted into the jumper along with the wool. Nana had washed and brushed my hair countless times. This was the first time I'd ever touched hers.

The hair reminded me of Jordan – my first conversation with Nana after my grandparents and aunt had moved in with us. Nana and I were sitting on plastic foot stools in a brown-tiled bathroom. I was four and she was old. Steam was rising up from the buckets of hot water around us. My dark curls clung to my bare wet shoulders.

Her hair was neatly braided, the end long, thin and twisted to keep the plait in place without the need for elastics. It was the same way Baba Gagi had taught me to braid on my Aunt Suzy's waist-length ponytail. My nana was dressed in layered white clothes that the moisture had melted into the folds in her arms and stuck to her wide belly. As she washed my hair, she told me about my father and his siblings – twelve children she had bathed all on her own. I didn't completely understand that my father had been a child or had been specifically *her* child, but I saw how the grown-ups fell quiet whenever she spoke. She was gentle with my hair. Her short square nails more pleasant on my scalp than my mother's pretty long ones. Once my hair was rinsed she pulled me in close and I could tell she was going to be sharing a secret. Her voice became hushed and her top lip sunk down to cover the gap between her two front teeth. She told me that I had to be nice to my Aunt Suzy because her real mother had died birthing her. I didn't know how a woman gave birth, but the conversation seemed too important for questions. My nana had taken Suzy in, raised her as her own. I remember wondering whether Suzy knew this secret. It felt big and I was worried the words wouldn't fit in my head and would come spilling out of my mouth once we left the bathroom.

When she had first moved in, Aunt Suzy was given my *dargushtah*, Baba Gagi was given the *kahnapah* and I was wedged into the middle of my parents' bed. Sleeping between two adults meant less room. My elbows were always bumping against a firm back or digging into a bloated belly. I would pull the sheets over my face to block out their snoring, my nose close to the fabric breathing in my mother's perfume Opium by Yves Saint Laurent. Rich and musky. In and out slowly until the spicy notes tingled in my throat and the hot air made my face sweat. In my dreams I would kick out trying to make space only to have my feet tickled into retreat by hairy arms and legs. My father would wake up with bruises and joke that I was playing soccer in my dreams. I quickly discovered the best place to sleep was on the floor next to my grandmother: Close to her chest and wrapped in her meaty arms. At night, she smelt like the large rectangular blocks of rose oil soap that came in hessian bags from Shimal and the orange peels she rubbed on her hands. I fell asleep gently pinching at the loose skin on the inside of her elbow. In the morning, I slipped out and watched *Pumpkin Patch* on mute, eating the *gemar* and *moraba* my Baba Gagi had brought in large glass jars from Baghdad: thick cream, sweet and milky and homemade apricot jam. The apricots were soft and sticky orange pieces floating in a smooth golden syrup. I used a large silver spoon to catch and scoop them into flat bread covered in the cream, careful not to ding the spoon on the sides of the glass and wake up one of the sleeping adults. The hair on my arms stuck to my skin as the sandwich dripped down my wrists with every bite. I never learnt how to fold the end in as neatly as my grandfather. I ate the *gemar* and *moraba* sandwiches for two weeks straight until one morning standing in the kitchen, shirt lifted, holding my grumpy belly in my hands, I announced to my family that I thought the cream was too oily. My nana was the only one not to laugh.

The avocado toast was cold now and *Millionaire Matchmaker* had ended. There was a too-loud car ad playing: a big red 4-wheel making tracks in a muddy road that had been moistened with film set sprinklers. I wanted to call my grandmother and tell her everything I remembered, but my Assyrian wasn't good enough for the phone. I needed my hands to speak. I turned the TV off and pulled the jumper up over my belly and toward my face and took a deep breath. All I could smell was old musty wool. Up close I spotted another silver hair poking from the fabric, then another and another. Every stitch was twisted with a hair in place. I felt my arms beginning to itch, my neck growing hot. I pulled the jumper off completely, careful not to let the hair touch my face. I laid it down on the ground, then I laid myself down beside it and tried to remember the Assyrian word for apricot: *Mishmish? Mishmisheh? Khokha?*

Goldfish

Tasnim Alam

—

I turned the cool, steel knob to Unit 8. I covered my mouth and sneezed. The smell of frying, dried chilli always caused a war in my nose. This never happened in Bangladesh but then again we didn't have to cook in a bathroom sized shit hole back there. I closed the door behind me and made my way towards the remote.

'Don't turn the TV on.' My mum popped her head out of the other side of the wall separating the kitchen from the drawing room, her hair frizzed up on her head.

I tilted my head to the side. I must have picked it up from a cat. 'Why?'

My mum glanced at the hallway leading to her room. My dad must be in there. 'Your dad's father died.' I opened my mouth and closed it. We didn't have a goldfish so I didn't know where I'd picked this habit up from. But it always took over when I was surprised.

The last time I'd seen my grandfather he only had hair on the sides of his head and his tall frame hadn't yet shrunken like it should at ninety. I could still feel the cold water against my naked flesh. I'd looked up from my cousin telling me a story about limbs falling off to see him over me. I jumped out but before I could get away he whacked me with his walking stick. His next words had been muffled by chesty coughs. I rubbed my shoulder at the memory of a long ago healed bruise. I looked up to see my mum's sharp brown eyes. I smiled and she slowly walked back into the kitchen. I walked up to the remote and slid it into a drawer. He had been a strict man but his eyes had always squinted when he smiled.

Fat Man

Maya Ali

—

'Bro, what the hell is wrong with you, you bloody smashed the shit out of my car.'

'*Allah yel3anak ya ibin al haram.*' My mum's eyes were open, her eyebrows crooked on top of her brown eyes. Dad stopped the car, his hands covering his cheeks leaning on the car window.

'*Shoubon* these people, *hadlon majnounin.*' The fat man looked in our direction with Adidas jacket and pants, hairy brown hands with the fluffiest black beard. The other fat man looked the same, with a black sweater accompanied with black pants, although a smaller black beard and curly hair.

Fat Man Number 1 was furious, his pale face turned red, it reminded me of my mum's tomato paste. Fat Man Number 2 looked like he was gonna get physical with his flobby stomach, leaning on the car door screaming at Fat Man Number 1. The Arabs around us walked with fear in their faces, as they looked shocked with their mouths slightly opened. Tired men came out of their packed manoush shops that smelled like meat and grilled cheese. They walked towards the fat duo, cars were beeping and the sun was going down. The fat men looked hungry and furious, grey smoke coming out of the bent metal in front of the cars. After a whole day of fasting, from their faces and their actions it seemed they couldn't handle it.

Fat Man Number 1 closed his car door roughly. 'I'm gonna call these guys, I know that can deal with this shit.'

Fat Man Number 2 looked up at him relieved. 'Alright *yallah*, I'm gonna wait.'

My dad turned the car around the outside of the road to continue the way back home.

'Mum?'

She looked at me with one eyebrow raised, 'Yes Maya?'

'What are we having for *ftoor* today?'

Thirteen Ways of Looking at a Pen

Kane Harrington

—

I hold the pen in my hand
Feeling the sturdiness
As if it could hold a 100 story tower

The pen is my sword
Its tip as sharp as a blade
The sabar drawing ink of blue blood

Why does it get lost?
Kicked on the ground
Underneath desks

Its tip
Chewed and worn
An old pacifier

Dashing across my page
Leaving a trail of blue
A bright vivid blue

As I continue to write
I feel the pen become a part of me
Printing my very soul

My paper becomes tainted
With a poison
A poison known as ink

The ink is inerasable
Just like the past
Mistakes have been made
Mistakes cannot be changed

With a simple click it is activated
A long tireless day of repeatability
Its days always the same

Stashed in a pencil case
In the darkness it resides
Prepared for anything

As time goes on
These simple pieces of plastic
Are replaced by computerised pens

The pen is like a rainbow
Erupting a plethora of dazzling colours

Oh no, the ink has run out
It has run its course
Now it's time for you to be replaced...

Pearly Blacks

Gabriella Florek

———

When the wind has finally brought her home from her play in the sun, my sister stands confidently in her chubby little frame upon the living room table and begins to dance. Knees bent, bottom jutting out, she moves side to side in a simple Latin two-step, eyes closed as though she is in silent meditation.

I peer at her through a crack in the living room door. The smell of fried beef mixed with onion and fresh tomato fill the air and I pray to our Spanish-speaking God (who has a furry face and large brown hands) that Mum doesn't see me hovering around the living room door ajar. Spying on your sister isn't a good enough excuse to have the house smelling of saltado.

I try to pick out the music in her head. Something our dad would play on repeat, a Susana Baca rhythm where Susana summons the Afro Peruvians to a call and response amidst a strumming charango. My sister holds her hands up to the sky and tilts her head back. She is in the throes of laughter. And balanced on the outstretched palm of her right hand, a rotting, black little molar sits defeated – silent and unmoving. I remember how long it took for that uncoordinated hand to be able to finally catch and throw, hit and slap. Now it is chubby and completely still. The molar stands upright as though it has placed its roots in my sister's hand and sprung up from her sweaty skin – a black thing clawing into her like a beetle with spiny legs. This is no accident. For months, I'd seen my younger sister carefully brushing all her teeth with the same love and dedication, except for a single molar in the back left-hand corner of her mouth. My grandmother, who we only ever call Abuela, cursed my sister for neglect, and swore at her in Spanish before taking out her dentures for a torrent of toothless abuse. This display was meant to frighten her, 'Look what you will become – a witch without teeth, *una bruja sin dientes*', but all it seemed to do was strengthen my sister's resolve.

Mum won't admit that Abuela knows something is afoot before her. Once she finds out about my sisters' rotten tooth, she will turn to my father. 'It's all that lemon with sugar you let them eat.' She won't admit she has the recipe down in her cookbook, a simple way to please us kids. Good mums don't glue their children's teeth together with sugar, and she'll go to the grave denying she ever did.

Mum would cut the lemon in half with the big knife from the draw, with that dexterity and command that told the world she owned the kitchen. The lemon would stand face down, waiting for the sweet, white granules to be measuredly poured beside it. The trick is to squeeze the lemon slightly when dipping it into the sugar, so that the juice breaks through the flesh, and the sweet stuff sticks faster. Then it's clenched-up faces and eyes rolling into the back of your head and sneaking more sugar onto the plate until the juice of the lemon is gone.

From the upside-down room at the other side of the house, I can hear my Abuela crying. She arrived from the other side of the world smelling like leather and talcum powder and I wonder if she always smelt that way. The foot of the bed blocks the door to the upside-down room so you can never open it all the way; you have to stick your head right around to say hello. If you lie upside-down on the bed, head facing the window, you can see the jacaranda flowers falling from the sky. I imagine my Abuela lying on her bed the right way up, her small, shrivelled body stretched out so that she is touching the window frame with her alpaca wool socks, even though it is summer. She has no interest in the purple flowers – she is waiting to be comforted, waiting to hear that she was right about my sister's tooth all along. As though my mum has heard her weeping, the sizzling from the saltado gets louder – she starts the stove fan.

Eyes on my sister, I am concentrating all my energy on her chubby little fingers squeezing the tooth in triumph. The door squeaks. My sister stops, looks me straight in the eye and smiles; her blood-stained canine smile. But there's a reason why you shouldn't smile and dance at the same time. Dancing is not for celebration – it's for mourning. Susana Baca and her African troupe could tell you that.

I watch my sister, legs spread, pigeon toed, and bottom out, ready to go again. She shuts her eyes, the rhythm in her head starting over, still smiling. I see it before it happens. The tooth slips from her fingers and she scrambles to catch it. She falls hard, face on table. I hear frying from the kitchen, crying from the upside-down room. My sister lifts her curly head up and as she does a shower of perfect baby teeth fall to the floor. I imagine the brown-handed God contemplating me from above. I laugh, relieved – the falling of my sister's teeth will mean I've stopped her from falling somewhere worse; from her bike, from the jacaranda or into the water that she is just learning to tolerate.

Ayat Al Kursi

Ushna Fatima

—

The light went off and the darkness was the only visible thing I could see. I looked out of my window and saw all of the houses in darkness as well. I could hear the clock ticking in the background, my mum saying go back to bed and my sister's frozen body staring at me with a blank face. I turned around and saw my youngest sister sleeping peacefully. I lay back down on my bed so I could sleep. I turned my head and saw a bright white light shining from my mum's phone and then turned my head and saw darkness.

I asked my mum what the time is and she replied back, 'It is 12am and you should sleep.' I started to hear a light sound of someone trying to kick the front door. Slowly and slowly, the sound started to get louder and louder.

That's when my mum asked me, 'Can you hear the sound?'

I replied, 'Yes!' The sound stopped but my heart was still beating fast. I tried to forget what happened but the thought could not get out of my mind. My mum told me to read *Ayat Al Kursi* so I could forget that heart racing moment and go to sleep. I started to read it but my words were stuttering. Slowly and slowly I started to feel normal. My heart started to beat at its normal pace and I was in peace. I closed my eyes and thought it was okay.

Lahme

Yazmeen Akoum

—

When me and Adam were both finished getting dressed we walked to the manoosh shop. As I walked in, the clear plastic curtain thingy smacked me in the face and made my nose numb. As I opened my eyes I saw Mr Muscles, his freshly cut beard and his eyebrow slit.

'I'll have one *lahme* with cheese.' Adam looked at me and mumbled something.

'Make that two please,' I said.

'Yew wont *lahme* and *jeben*?' he said in a woggy accent. That butterfly feeling in my stomach was leaving slowly.

'Yes please,' I said.

'We no have *lahme*, you wont *jeben*?'

I was disgusted his accent made me forget about his freshly cut beard and his built muscles. He came out of the register area to show me what the *jeben* looked like. He was wearing black and white stripy leggings and pink thongs. I left the shop midway of him speaking to me.

Work Fucked Up My Life

Aqeela Shauab

—

6am and I get a call from George in a voice that sounds like an import Santa Clause. I have plans so after he fucks up my sleep I get up out of my warm cosy bed and into the cold filled bathroom. I wash my face with steaming water and brush my teeth with minty paste. I get dressed out of the clothes that made me look homeless and into clothes that look not so homeless. I get picked up in a shit-box Holden with a friend I've known for two years. He's the typical Punchbowl bloke with his shitty high-top haircut, beard, Gucci hat, Adidas bumbag and Nike Air Maxes doing shitty burnouts.

Bullshit Delusions

Samantha Hogg

—

My sprained ankle throbs, propped up on some pillows and covered with a bag of thawing peas, soaking the fabric and so fucking cold compared to the ridiculous summer night. Sweet, sweet painkillers are starting to kick in, my eyes are heavy and I feel like I'm floating, fucking ankle still hurts though, drugs really don't fix everything.

The cat's snoring too loud and kicking his little feet as he dreams. I hate him right now. You little shit, you could at least come and cuddle your perpetually injured mum. He's stretched out on the floor, impossibly long for such a small thing, refusing to get on the bed because it's too hot and he kind of hates me back.

My broken ass fan creaks and rattles as it sways back and forth, pushing hot air at me instead of doing its damn job and the yellow lights from my modem throw shadows over the walls, making my eyes hurt until I focus on them properly, only to regret it immediately. Faces and clawed hands appear with every flash, a twinge of fear jolts through me like a wet powerpoint. I don't need this right now.

I can feel myself getting twitchy, anxiety taking control of my nervous system. This is going to get way worse before it gets better.

Yep, here we go, here comes the horrorshow shitstorm. It starts with an out of place noise to my right, a shadow without a source, and now there are disembodied people in my room. I can hear them breathing, feel them watching me, their footsteps as loud as the YouTube video I left on to sleep to. How does something without fucking form breathe or walk? Same with the staring tbh. What the fuck is up with that? You don't have eyes, how can you stare at me with such judgement?!

Logically I know there's no one there, myself and the cat are the only living creatures in the room (well, there's the plants too, but when do plants ever count?). I can hear them over my favourite screaming men playing video games, that unexplainable static hum that tells me we're not alone, it's distracting as all hell. I'm tired and high, fuck off.

The shadows and sounds are already planting ideas in my gullible, anxiety-ridden mind. Rapid fire memories of childhood (and adulthood) fears flash through my mind like a lightspeed projector, everything's out to get me now.

(My mother's rotting arms reaching for me; 'They're here!' Strangers' faces grinning through the windows; 'Demon! Give me a name!' A man that can kill me in my dreams is waiting patiently; 'I see dead people.' Don't think about possessed trees... or dolls... or people. Just y'know what, don't think about possession).

All those horror movie creatures I'm so fascinated by are after my blood, every fucking thing I've ever been afraid of is coming out at once. I can't... something's wrong, my heart's beating too fast, I'm going into cardiac arrest, I need a doctor, I'm going to die, someone help me for the love of fuck. My throat's too tight, I can't breathe like there's something caught in there, a piece of food I can't swallow around, when did I eat last, could something have been stuck in my teeth this whole time?

My hands clench until I feel my palm bleed beneath a broken nail, digging my too-long fingernails in deeper because through pain there is clarity. My wise mind, which sounds a lot like my therapist, tells me it's just hallucinations and anxiety. Simone whispers to be mindful, reach out with your senses, what's in the room for sure, facts not feelings. She also says, 'Seriously? Stop hurting yourself!' But my brain don't give a fuck about being wise or mindful, I'm too fucking scared and the pain helps, Simone!

They're by the head of my bed and I swear I feel the bed dip slightly as though someone is climbing onto it, where's the fucking cat, gotta explain it away. Holding my head still, I look around for the furry little prick. He's still stretched out on the floor, he hasn't made a move to jump on to the bed, little bastard is snoring even louder now. I want to run but can't, my ankles so swollen I can't even put the blanket over it, where would I go if I could?

I try to control my breathing, in through the nose and out through my mouth, cool air in, warm air out. Inhale 'wise,' exhale 'mind'. Repeat until you feel calm... Repeat until you feel calm... Repeat until... Fuck this. Fucking hallucinations. Fucking cockbite ghosts.

Fuck it, I'll just get up and have a smoke and a Valium.

On the Way Home

Sam Sabri

—

/ *If the Father*

If the Father
is your Brother
then who is the Sister
Father
of the Mother of your Sister
going to be?

/ Azar Boys

On the way home the weather was hot and there was no clouds as it was very sunny. When we arrived home Mum asked us how was the day. We told her 'everything.'

The next day to school we met our friends and when the bell went TTTNN we went to class. We had Science.

Our Science teacher ask, 'Does bat get baby by eggs or by birth?' Everyone in the class said eggs except for me I say birth and I actually got it right. We all started to laugh and everyone started to copy whatever I say.

Science teacher asked another question saying, 'Does the snake get babies by laying eggs or by birth?' I said birth and people copy me but I got it wrong and Science teacher started to laugh.

When the day ended me and my brothers got out of school to go back home. There was some Azar people that looked much older. They were wearing big black jumpers. Their face was scary because there was a lot of scratches and there was a lot of lines. There was three of them Azar. When we walked past they call my brother Samer.

Said to my brother, 'Give me any food or money that you got on you right now.'

Samer say, 'I don't have anything.'

Then one guy pulled a knife out and he tried to stab Samer. Me and my brothers started to fight them. One of my family friend Mohamed came and broke the fight. He picked us up in his car and drove us home. We tell him everything that happened. Same with our mum. Mum decided to get a driver to pick us up from school. She had to pay him twenty dollars a week. Foud, our driver, was very kind person but his car looked ugly and it stopped in middle of road always. Foud's car couldn't drive up hills because it was really slow.

╱   *This Eye*

When I was young I used to call the train bus and the bus train but they are opposite. I thought that the bullet of a gun looked like a ball from this eye to this eye. Thank god!

Gunfire in Midnight

Aws Al Khamisi

—

When I was a child in Iraq Myssan, everyday I go to my school, which is actually not a big one. It has a small classes and cafeteria and a playground. Sometimes I get bulled by the students cuz of my religion. I get angry and sometimes I start punching them then when the bell rings I come back home from school because it's really close to my house and when I go to sleep I get jumpscared because of the gunfire in midnight that happens. I thought these people who are shooting are going to break our door and start shooting us. Me, my dad, mum and my sister went by car to Jordan. There where my cousin family welcomed us into their house and taught us everything we needed to know about Jordan.

Last Gift

Azeez Azeez

—

Before many years in Baghdad, I was living in my home with my parents, in my birthday I was very happy and even my parents were very happy because I am the only son for them. My mother told me that we have a guest who will visit us. I told her who, she told me your father's uncle.

I was preparing to my birthday, my father's uncle came with my father. He was a goldsmith living in Erbil in the north of Iraq. He was a tall man blumb little bit. Once I saw him I went up and he shake my hand. He told me happy birthday and gave a small box. He told me this your gift. After a few hours my father's uncle went with my father to the station to catch a bus to got back to Erbil. I opened the box and I saw a very nice watch hand. It was green. After a few days I hear from my parents that my father's uncle dead because of the war. Once I heard that I become more close to my watch and whenever I see it I remember my father's uncle. I saw him only one time but his gift always makes me remember.

The First Day of Ramadan

Belal Shahoud

—

/　*Donkey*

I drank a cup of beer
after a hour
felt myself like
donkey walking on street

/ After I Finished Praying

I wake up at 10:44am. I went to the bathroom to get *wadu*. I washed my hand three times and wash my nose and put water in my mouth and spit it out. When I finished I went back to my bedroom to pray. My bedroom had my bed and my brother bed and my computer. I asked my mum which way is kabba. I started to pray.

I put my hands up and I said, '*Allah akber.*'

After I finished praying I went to play on my computer. I played like two three hours. After I finished I went downstairs to living room where very big in the wall there was a Quran and oclock and my old brother picture when he was little and the TV table on there was small TV and my school books under. My mum were sitting on the sofa I sat next to her. She were watching TV show called *Babalhuaria*. It's an old TV show like hour half. I felt like I'm sleeping in the sofa so I went back to my room to sleep. I turned the fan on in put in front of face because it was summer and hot. I close my eyes to sleep but I couldn't because it was really hot. I tried to close my eyes again. I sleep like one or more but I don't remember.

I wake up around 4:44pm. I was very hungry but it's not the way to break our fast. I smell the smell of the delicious food that my mum was preparing. I went to the kitchen asked Mum what she cooking for us she said, 'Noodles and *lahma bí samiy.*'

At 7:35pm me and my old sister were getting the table ready. All my family sitting down around waiting for *adan*. When we were starting to eat we heard a boom voice sound real bad my older sister start to cry and scream.

Mum screaming, 'Mohoumd!'

I didn't know what I should do so I run upstairs to see what's wrong. I screamed, 'Mohoumd, where are you?'

I heard I was sayin, 'I'm alright go down.'

Me my family and three uncle run down to my uncle shop because the tank were shooting next to us. My uncle shop were very away from the streets. We sat around, we all were, my and brother and Mohoumd run upsteps to get water bottle, we get three bottle and saw smoke coming out of my room but I didn't went because the tank shouting. We have to run so no one get hurt. We down to shop we saw my dad and uncle standing around and talking. They said we should move from here from tomorrow.

All the kids went to sleep at 9pm with the tank still shouting.

On the morning we saw my dad and mum preparing a big bag that has our money inside and my uncle same. We jumped to a big van and then we run away from our house to different village.

But I still remember our house from five years ago and see our house from that time.

Iran Syria

Ghadeer Darraji

———

/ *Bullet Out*

Dad would try to hide the weapons why because I used to play with guns. Hide the guns. Take the bullet out of the guns put them back. I was the only boy in the family so he wouldn't hurt me. Once in Iran my dad got a gun from his friend. My dad's friend was a scary cop. My dad gets all kinds of weapons. Days later I heard knocking on the door and six army people and they check my house for guns. They kept following me so they didn't find anything. They said thank you for letting me check our house.

/ Marks

At school in Syria it was very very hot. As probably most of you know in the Middle East the weather is about thirty-five degrees. At school I had a history test and I failed. I got fifteen out of twenty. My teacher was really tough. Man, he had a big belly, a weird 90s moustache and thick black hair. He was holding a big wooden stick with his big hands. He gave us the marks. Then he called the names of the people that failed told them to stand up front in a line. Lucky me, I was at the back. He started slapping us. '*Ya haiwanat!*' He leave us mark on our faces and hands. The bell rang and we went to recess. We forget what happened before. My friends Mohammed, Tem and Bilal found a bottle of Coke and we started kicking it around cause no one had a real soccer ball or they do but can't bring it to school. Mohammed is short and so fast. We couldn't catch him while he run. As I sat down to rest I heard a big sound. A missile hit my school and exploded on the roof. Stun and panic I ran really fast to the front of school so my parents will come get me. But the teacher so dumb he didn't let us wait for our parents. People fighting trying to get inside outside and when I tried the teacher slap me across the face. I got angry and kick the teacher in his private part and I opened the door and escaped.

Forget All Things

Sam Nathim Naeem

—

/ *Tshek*

Before seven years when I live in Baghdad with my family. I have twin brother and one sister. It was so hot and my father get to go visit him brother. We all go. When we start to walk we hear some sound from the east. It was a rocket and it was like this tshek. We start to run back to home but my father friend, who live near our house, so said our home destroy. All our things still inside. We went away with only the clothes we wear.

We stay at my uncle home. We stay with him for years and years. He gave my father a job. After two years we went to get flat in some place called Korkok. So we forget all things.

/ Ripe Move

dug dug swim in river
tell the fish the net coming
moving from and save your
self in the ripe move

/ The Gone

We gone from our country the one we left in
as the bird flying but never come back
and the reason for the gone has no end

/ Donkey

When I was young I thought donkey same as Azmal

Hard Days

Saman Al Zuhairi

—

/   *Cuz*

I was in a hard days. Was in school. My school start from 12pm to 5pm. Everyday I run away from it or jump over the fence just to run away from it. Everyday I run away with Bashar, Mohamed and my cuz Mohamed.

/   *Forget*

When you are away I got fat
forget you and then in last
shot found you in the
cucumber and yoghurt

/   *Salty*

no ship head
no bread and soup
and not even salty cucumber

Covered Us

Savyo Yonan

—

My family three beds were empty. Only me. I heard gun shooting. It sounded like really heavy rain. I got up. Running through the hallway with my family's pictures on the walls. Pictures of when my parents married and when me and my brother were born. In the living room I saw my mum, she turns on the grey TV watching the news. My brother was sitting next to my mum on the blue couch waiting for me. Then my mum grab me and my brother laid us down on the white floor and covered us with a blue blanket just in case they shoot our house. There was a black Syria helicopter. There was a soldier wearing black armour shooting a mini gun.

The Old Days in Syria

Adam Alsabahi

—

/ *Onion*

I feel I am crazy
I am eating onion
thought it was lolly

/ *Abraham, Salah and Wisam*

It was awesome. The old days in Syria. Me, Abraham, Salah and Wisam was playing soccer not far from our house. We made the goals by using rocks. We make the soccer of papers or bottle of water. We play next to a supermarket too. It was a small shop but it had everything drinks and food. There was an old man working in the shop. Every time we playing he bring a chair and sit outside in front of his small shop to watch. Sometimes we go buy drinks or something to eat and after that we go play PlayStation or computers.

Carrying my Father

Ameer Alkhamis

—

I was helping my father in our gold shop. Our house was vis-à-vis with our shop. One woman came in and started shouting that all of the gold was for her. Everyone say, 'She crazy don't care.' We close the shop for a few hours.

A few days later the same woman come back with four or five men like gang. My three uncles came to help my father deter this gang. The gang went but promised they'd be back. After a few days one policeman came to our shop, give my father a paper and said it was from the courts. My father fell down. I was going two steps forward shouting and making people come help my father. I went back two steps carrying my father. My uncles and mother and my brothers carried my father to the hospital. When my father felt better he went to the court and the judge was knowing right.

The judge said the woman should stay in prison five years but she was pregnant and got out.

After seven or eight months my parents were out for a wedding. Just my brother and I were in the home playing PlayStation. I heard a big car noise.

After that I heard knocking at our front door and someone shouting, 'They killed your nephew!'

Outside police was everywhere and they took my cousin to the hospital. He has three shots in his head. The same gang which came to us before killed my cousin and took his gold and money.

Bak Mandi

Adam Phillip Anderson

—

I walk off the plane at Ngurah-Rai Airport in Denpasar, Bali. Incense in the night air smells like flowers and tobacco. It's close to midnight and my head-hair sticks to my forehead and neck as I cross the tarmac.

Mock-ancient *candi bentar* gates mark the passages to the terminal. These *candi bentar* are made of red-brick, like pagodas flattened then split in two to make a grand portal. Inside the terminal, the shrill melody of a suling flute soars over brisk bamboo keys. I cross through the arrivals building, past a colourful bust of Garuda in humanoid-eagle form to the station of a Balinese customs officer. His forehead, under close-cropped black hair, is dark and smooth like stained wood. His lean, clean-shaven jawline and unblemished skin makes it difficult to tell if he's twenty-one or forty.

'Welcome to Indonesia,' he says to his ink-stamp.

'*Selamat malam*,' I say, '*Ini paspor saya.*'

'*Dari mana?*' he asks calmly while examining my passport. His voice is dull compared to the frantic, dizzying finale of the gamelan.

'*Dari* Australia *Pak.*'

I pay twenty-five US dollars for a Visa on Arrival, retrieve my luggage and exit toward the domestic terminal. With a few hours left until my flight to Java, I find a quiet corner under the terracotta roof of an open-air lobby, behind a granite *Bedogol* statue. I examine the four-legged gate guardian's bulging eyes and toothy grimace, it looks like one of the tougher enemies from *Final Fantasy*. At its feet sits a small *Canang Sari*, offering yellow frangipanis, patchouli leaves and jasmine flowers in a thin tray of young bamboo.

Dropping my sixty-litre backpack on the floor, I lay my sweaty head on the bag and think about my extended family's home in Yogyakarta, where I am heading now. Our house sits a few narrow, motorbike congested streets into an urban village. When I stay, I sleep in a loft above Kakek, my mum's father, near the bathroom and Nenek's kitchen. Geckos and stray cats frequent the corrugated tin roof and the dark corners of the room are home to mice and mosquitoes. The stairs to my loft are steep, like a ladder, to save space. At the foot of the stair-ladder is a mountain of shoes belonging to Kakek, Nenek, my two aunties, uncle, my cousins and me. The whole time, I was the biggest cry-baby. I cried when I was tired from jetlag. I cried when Mum forgot to tell the *pedagang bakso* not to add green onion to my soup. I cried because I had to eat mi goreng with a spoon because Nenek didn't have any forks. I kicked and screamed and had snot dripping down my chest when I had to use the bathroom. It was a squat toilet with no paper and with coarse, chipped tiles on the floor and walls. There was only a dim light from a small, decades-old, brass oil lamp. The *bak mandi* was full of undrinkable water because tiny worm-like mosquito larvae made the *bak mandi* their home. The *gayung* handle was encrusted in filth.

One morning, my nenek found me watching TV alone in the *ruang duduk*.

'*Mandi*,' she said, after seeing my thick head of dandruff.

I knew it meant shower, but I pretended I didn't. I feigned the wide-eyed, hopeless concentration of someone who wanted to understand. Nenek had fair skin for a Javanese woman but her broad flat nose gave away her heritage. The wrinkles around her eyes were the mark of a long life of caring for others. She clutched a calico bag full of fruits, vegetables and chillies from the market and removed her hijab, which she always took off her head when she was at home, revealing a small, wiry bun of greying hair. Not wanting to disobey my mum's mum, I grabbed my towel, toothbrush and some bottled water for rinsing my mouth. After finding my rubber thongs in the shoe mountain, I hesitated at the bathroom door, looking in. '*Ayoh*,' said Nenek, walking by me and into the kitchen with a large pot under her arm. She waved for me to enter with her free hand.

I brushed my teeth and wet my hair. In the next room, Nenek was frying tempe and singing along to a *dangdut* casette. I poured water from the *gayung* into the toilet and then a few times onto the floor making a loud, deliberate whoosh so it would seem like I was pouring it over my body.

I hoist my bag back onto my shoulders and walk towards a toilet sign, passing a group of three *taksi* drivers. Two lean on their cars, the other squats nearby. The squatter has a thin moustache with a *batik* cloth covering his head. One of the leaners is smoking a *Gudang Garam*.

The three look at me like an easy fare before I pre-emptively say, '*Tidak terima kasih.*' They seem disappointed for a moment before they spot two singlet-clad *orang bule* approaching from a distance, surfboard bags in hand. One singlet has the Bintang logo, the other, Rip Curl.

Inside the toilet cubicle I hang my bag on a hook and squat down. The smell of *Gudang Garam* reminds me of Kakek, my mum's father. I think of one evening in particular, when I was eighteen and Kakek was seventy-four. We sat on plastic chairs behind Nenek's kitchen smoking cigarettes, slapping mosquitoes from our ankles. While waiting for the *Alllllaaaaaahu Akbar* of the call to prayer to resonate across the village, Kakek squinted his eyes to read the health warning on the pack of cigarettes I bought with me from Australia. 'Smocking... cawsses... blyndness,' he pronounced with heavy breath. 'I am smoke Dutch cigarette since I am nine!' he laughed, showing me his gold and maroon pack of *Gudang Garams*. They crackle when you inhale them and I asked him why. He scratched his thin white hair and mustache, formulating his response in English. 'Netherland people, when they come they can't lighting the cigarette, so they put gunpowder inside.' He laughed again, but I wasn't sure at what, but whenever he laughed, I knew it came from Sumatran hinterland to the durian trees of Papua, finally settling here in middle Java to plant seeds, which became my mother.

I finish in the bathroom, cleaning myself from the *gayung* for real this time. Back outside, the *taksi* drivers are rushing the two tired-looking White boys. Rip Curl says, 'Koota Beach,' repeatedly. Hearing the words 'Kuta Beach' makes my back sweat and my scalp itchy. I had been there once, at eighteen, on a layover returning from Yogyakarta to Australia with my dad. Kuta consists of a commercial strip along the coastline of a bay. If you stand still on the strip, an American or Australian tourist will push you aside; if you walk around, Indonesians will offer you motorbikes, Balinese girls or magic mushrooms.

I remember one group of hustlers when I was walking around with my dad, who had spent some time convincing me to leave our hotel room. He knew his money weighed more here and was always looking to make the most of it. Dad wore polarised sunglasses and a grey polo over football shorts and thongs, which exposed his distinct sock-tan. The two skin tones on his legs contrasted like a block of Cadbury Top Deck. He usually wore long pants so Indonesians wouldn't call him a Dutch, but on the Kuta strip he could be tall and pale without a second thought. He and I strolled through a back street and found a troop of *mbak-mbak*. Wait, they were Balinese girls, so I guess they're just called *gadis*. They were *nongkrong*-ing by a white stone wall, chatting like pigeons. They wore thin, baggy shirts and short-shorts. Some had white jasmine flowers in their black hair from a nearby tree. Seeing the exposed hair was a far cry from the Muslim women of Java.

The girls stopped chatting and asked if I wanted massage.

'*Tidak terima kasih*,' I said.

They asked if I wanted some mushroom and I said the same again. As we approached the Kuta strip I took earphones from my shorts and played myself some black metal. 'I've boarded myself inside, I refuse to exit!' screamed Deafheaven's frontman over a storm of stiff-wristed guitars. I side-stepped surfboard Whites as we passed by a Burger King, a pirate DVD shop and a Circle K convenience store.

'Let's go to the beach,' said Dad, pulling out one of my earphones.

'You can,' I said, putting it back in.

He shrugged and wandered through the *candi bentar* gates that stood between the strip and the beach. This portal was taller than most and made of dark stone that had turned green in patches from the ocean salt. It had *Bedogol* guardians near the base, where four or five dreadlocked surfers passed around a longneck of beer. As the last note of the black metal song rung out, tinnitus in my ears gave way to an airy, head-bopping jazz flute melody. I turned three-sixty, looking for its source. One of the white water Whites had produced a portable speaker. 'For my people in the front, front. In the nosebleed section, section,' ad-libbed one of the rappers from Hilltop Hoods. *The Hindu spirits of Kuta Beach have been overthrown by ghosts in muscle-shirts*, I thought. *The songs and rituals have become Hilltop Hoods and Bintang Pilsener.*

Finally, the gate opens for my flight to Yogyakarta. As I sweat my way back across the tarmac, all I can think about is grabbing that filthy *gayung* and having a good, long *mandi*.

Shababs

Dani Mejbel

—

It was on the 25th of January in 2013 in Sweden. It was a ice cold night when me, my best friend Alex and my brother Sameer went out one night to an abandoned area. Alex was my first friend. It was a big day for all the Mandaeism community because we had Eid.

Florent

Jason Gray

—

Fragments of whistling sand
upon breezy, matted mounds,
sewn by rising oceans,
I am bustled, hustle dreams.

Dozing, counting clouds,
coconut flakes. Barren mountains drifting,
head on Nana's hunched shoulder,
KFC-ad lullabies. Red letter daze.

—

Hurried entrance, Uno/Ludo wizards @ Grand Baie,
Papa sister's bungalow breeze,
bent palm trees. Pebblecrete: *honk!*
Road rage @ Castle Hill. Driveway, ambulance.

Catatonic, hospital waiting room,
cold veiny hands, tubes, grandparents watch the green flat line,
Awake! I am bleak sunshine.
No boat trip, #Rodrigues.

What is #Mauritius without parents, anyway?
Aman! iPod shuffle, sugar
and glass museums.
Taxi driver waits without air-con.

Tears in the bistro under the ceiling fan.
Jug of Coca-Cola, ice. Spillage
on the floral white, frills and napkins,
'Eat, eat, babies!'

Giant macarons and achard, no salad.
Nana avec sister Matilda in the sega dress,
twin cultures, blue and white, floral.
Younger sibling, wiser for some reason.

Escape! Scorsese montage. Mental,
driven, eat more: coconut juice, dholl puri.
Success! Seize ans! Time to fly. 'Florent!'
Nana instructs, 'Girls everywhere, bebe!'

—

'Um... what's the deal with the Y2K bug?'
I say to the concierge,
peach hotel dress, Coke bottle glasses,
Perfect Creole and French, broken English.

This ruddy chipmunk teleported,
Archipelagic Magic, skin of our arms bubbling,
in the hammock, head curls
unruly, madness in dreadlocked time.

Drop a selfie with Anju, inert. *Flash!*
A moment stolen, fresh for brain-scoop-agram.
Phone to muddy Rosehill turf,
Mum's distant swimming hole, gene pool.

Volleyball captain, scholar,
took us to South Cronulla and The Entrance,
and reminds us that she can't swim,
and reminds me she can't fly, not that way.

Anju grabs my phone — sticky Anglo, scurry
hearts on our round-cheeked smiles
in boxes, behind screens —
and puts it down her dress.

I excuse myself, cheap case
of Phoenix beers, esky ice, ignore thigh vibration.
Arrive late to the table, sedate, eyeballs still,
but in one shaking piece, cut-off jeans.

—

Foo Fighters T-shirt and Colorados
bought for work experience
at Castagnet Lawyers,
'Prawn *rougaille, faratha*, only. *Merci*.'

In the specious sun, procrastinating,
more memes and poses
and Facebook posts,
more trips to crystalline waters and feasts.

And sterile shonky Westerners clogging
and hollering on the bistro dancefloor,
howling at the mirror-ball. Faeces! Sparkling fess-pee, sa.
Damages on TV, I hate that stinkin' ass show.

I cleanse in the bistro basin, water beads on hot sweat.
Nana is chirpy and assured,
'Phone buzz, no fuss!' Laughs.
I cave, more biryani and chicken curry, 'Co-ka-coh-la?!'

I squirm in my seat, Creole and French rain,
I pocket-mash. Phone sa, that aching device,
HURLS random kazoo melody,
@ the whole Grand Baie bistro, @ sega for the tourists.

I hit hashtag intruder, hit American cat,
paws, jump-cutting, paws and blue-grey stare,
Da-der-der-da-da-der-der-dada-dada-der.
I register floppy plush oversized earphones,

exactly like Dad's costume hat for Tonton's parties.
Room stops, stares, I hit my own phone screen in terror.
'FLORENT!'
all Nana says, mock outrage,

'Ayo, bubba!' echoes, unsaid,
incredulous eyebrows jiggling
up forehead creases, grinning piano mix,
rotten and false teeth. So lovely

stampede, music continues, voluntourists
sent to party, quell White Working Class rebels.
Sit my ass down. I am an internet cat, stuck
in jump-cuts, Dodo T-Shirt, beer, Creole bistro.

Tyreice Peachey

——

I'm a proud Indigenous man.

I always find a way to fuck up.

I've grown up in Glenmore Park since birth and it's always been happy and joyful but for the past years there's been bad things happening.

1.

I wake up, get ready, and go to school
All I do all day is learn and sit
I walk to Maccas grab a feed walk home

2.

Walking to go see my dad
A guy on a bike got hit by a car
We were fucking scared and rang the ambulance

3.

Driving to Frankies to grab ice in Samoa
Packing it in the boot for training
Toni then got hit by a car probably coz his Tongan

Brandon Gale

—

I'm proud to be Aboriginal
Ty is a great rugby player
I moved in Glenmore this year so far its been great

Marko Bogic

—

I have a large nose and I'm half Wog
Sean has a lot of freckles and is a little chubby
Warragamba I live in front of the bush and behind the road

This is the beginning, this is the middle and that is the...

Trinity Wensley

—

him: show me that pic ur showing everyone now?

me: what pic?

him: apparently ur showing everyone a pic of my dick to everyone i want to see coz i want to see

me: i don't have one?? what are you talking about?

him: coz trent told me that apparently showing a pic of my dick and trent's a great friend and i trust him

me: you believe that talk shit, not me coz it didn't come outta my mouth

———

I have fifteen siblings

Half:
levi
abbie
evie
ellie

Step:
tiarne
telise
jonah
kirsty
kawana
viley
beau
michael
will
khyle
kristen

Dominic Mills

—

'I'm gonna miss you,' I said.
'I will too,' Josh said.
'Why you gotta go?' I said.
'I have to,' Josh said.
'Bye bye I love you,' I said.
'I love you too,' Josh said.
He went to Kapooka.

———

I'm always moving around Australia

I have annoying neighbours

My dad works for the ADF / Australian Defence Force

Kasey Weightman

—

She woke up on a chilly morning and stumbled out of bed. She was still dizzy after last night. She dizzily walked out into the backyard and fell over into the white blanket of snow.

———

I stared at the other team, waiting for them to throw the ball over the net. The ball flew over the net and my attempt to catch it wasn't that good. A minute later, my finger was in pain and a few days later, I figured out it was fractured.

———

I yowled in pain as Socks scratched my leg. The tabby she-cat had left a lot of pain in my leg. A day or two later, I found out one of her claws was stuck in my leg.

Trenton Fynn

—

Round up the boys for an arvo.
Walk through the bush together.
FUCKING SNAKE!!!

—

Chillin in the caravan park,
darts on the floor. I go to Ollie and eat shit on the floor.

———

People in Warragamba love their cousins and extra toes aye.

———

Give us your dog.
Got a durry sebba.
Get out of the shed.

Samantha Snedden

—

We walked up King Street.
While I bitch about my legs.
We talked, we finally ate octopus & hot chips & I smiled.

I walked into my cousin's apartments at Redfern.
Seen a drunk guy laying with half of his
body out of the elevator, while the doors still try to close.

This year has been an emotional rollercoaster
and I can't wait for a new year.

———

I want Nat to bring me Subway.

———

After school I'm going to go Maccas and get a quarter pounder meal because today is pay day.

———

Sure thing chicken wing.

———

I met you, you intrigued me.
Made me smile.
Then left me.

———

Me and Nat sit at Nandos.
I eat and groan then laugh.
Shame you have no money.

Tellah Edwards

—

finally made it into year 12 also the first in my family to do so bitches

▬

i am obsessed with el jannah especially the garlic sauce and the chicken i fucking love it

▬

bitches
too many girls hatin cause they ain't so imma keep it humble

———

glenmore has never been the same since the gangs and violence. I feel unsafe in my own area.

———

Me and my sister Emily were watching TV she was eating cookies and I wanted one and she said no so I punched her in the face.

———

On Saturday I went to a party and there was so many people there within an hour of the party a brawl started so I started running and my phone fell out of my pocket and then some gronk stole it.

Riley Kefford

—

in the corner of my room there sat a tank. in that tank sat a frog that stared at a fly and licked its lips. the fly jump out the tank and flew right in the middle of my eyes.

▬

i was babysitting my cousins. i got the bath ready for them but they were missing. my cousin came in and said that my baby cousin had ran down the road naked.

when my sister was eleven she broke her arm she jumped off the shed roof and failed badly. all i saw was her snap bone and it was all purple and swollen.

i go to a shop and manage to come out with a full trolley.

Mr B i hate you so much because of your big fat ugly nose.

Warragamba is beautiful and quiet except for Christmas, Easter and Anzac Day and Halloween.

i love sushi, kebabs and chinese.

i hate Miss W because she is old and sour.

Lachlan Holmes

—

The players heading for the field, the game hasn't even started yet but it's already intense. Then the whistle blows and the ball goes flying through the air. Then the crowd cheers louder and louder then the ball collides with the wet. It's game over and everybody shouts out of the stadium.

———

I am kind of tall.
My dad has no hair.
Penrith Panthers for life!!!

———

My hair is blond
Some of my friends are jerks
There are some fights

Jamil Janif

——

Sometimes we wish we could be anyone or anything, someone or something but we can only be ourselves.

▬▬

I'm going to my friends' party on Friday and I'm getting a Border Collie.

Chelsea Randell

—

moments i took for granted

cloud watching, my favourite thing, an unusual day to go cloud-watching would be when there were no clouds right? but i mean laying on the grass in an almost empty field next to you is an even better feeling. laying there in complete silence cloud watching, with not one care or cloud in the sky and somehow you still made it feel momentous.

As I sit here on the deck, underneath the stars, watching them disappear late at night, I realised there weren't many people around, there were a few dazers and then it hit me. there were only two types of people up this late, people who were in love and people who were lost. I was a bit of both, I was in love and I was lost. I was in love with a boy, a boy who I knew would never love me back. he loved her, she was alive in the moment, free spirit kind of girl, I was not however. I was a planned out, cautious, self-conscious girl. this made me lost, I didn't know what to do with myself yet, I watched you love her. I watched you talk about her with the same passion that's in my eyes when I talk about you. I pretended I was happy for you, yet you broke me, you broke me so hard that anyone who came close to fixing me I ended up breaking them instead. I find it amazing that there are at least a million people all gazing up at the same stars, all thinking about a million different thoughts. one million thoughts were going through my head but they all happened to be about you, you... the one who my mood depended on. but what do I do if you're my everything, but I'm not even your something...?

Tahlia Blacklock, Kiah Bolt and Mikayla Kumar

—

the stars and the
moon tell the
stories of the
unknown

Mikayla Kumar

—

The sound of the rain on the window sings me to sleep as the warm doona holds me in a comforting cuddle. My mind refuses to remain silent. Thoughts run like an Olympian in a track race. I suddenly find myself groggy and warm, my alarm blaring and the sun piercing through the blinds that hang besides my bed.

Colt Currell

—

Things we do but do not know
Things we love but do not show
These things are a part of all of us as we grow
We are the generation to do our good
deeds, we are the generation to surpass hunger
& greed, we are the ones to save this
earth & help show its undoubtable worth.
I'm no inspirational speaker but I know what I
feel. Small things that make me happy like my music
class twice a week it makes me happy just to think all
these notes & these lines can make
something greater, another thing just riding
with mates it all helps me leave the cruel realities
behind & lets me unwind it so good it feels like a crime.

The abyss of endless darkness
ravaging through my body.

The visible smile upheld on my
face, a clear reminder of a rare occasion.

After several hours of chasing this pesty bird I hear a clang, it's
the sound of the
front door opening. I run to the door with a shot of excitement
through my bones & my tail going wild, I just knew they were
home the ones I love.

Hayley Laws

—

Set sail on the boat of imagination
The universe waits until you're ready & only then
the boat will depart.
Steer your imagination to beyond the universe.
Wait & the right boat will depart.
The right door will creak open but you have to
open it.
The sound of instruments help me escape.

Harrison Randell

——

My alarm clock walks in my room screaming louder than a jet taking off disappearing in the distance down the hallway. Tossing and turning to the side with the sun glaring through the creaks of my blinds. Pulling the blanket over my head. What feels like seconds turns into ten minutes, my alarm clock returns once more to my blankets off. The nightmare starts as I get ready to go to school.

Caitlin Laws

—

I wish it all went away!

Sometimes don't you just wish all the sickness and injuries were all gone, no-one laying in hospital bed staring at a blank ceiling, no-one getting hurt with bandages wrapped around their head, no-one doping up on medicine trying to make them better. No-one scrunching up their fist and throwing a punch, or taking off your shoe and throwing a kick. I wish there was no violence, I wish it all went away.

I walked up the wooden stairs, every step I took I heard a creak behind me on the right side. I looked up and seen the moon shining bright on my face. I kept walking. I reached my door, grabbed out the silver key and twisted the door open. As soon as I opened it, a whoosh of the cold night air went past my body, making the hairs on my neck stand up. I said to myself I'll go to sleep and hope it was all a dream.

Sometimes don't you wish that the anxiety went away with no-one worrying and stressing about the little things in life, no one being lonely walking around with a frown on your face?

Story: You look at the sunset and you see the beautiful combinations of the colours in the sky, I look into the clouds and feel calm and enjoy the different shapes and colours in the sky.

Question: What do you feel when you're looking up in the sky towards the sunset?

———

Just a story about the sunset cause I was bored.
I walk outside to get fresh air I look towards the
sky I thought it was nothing but I took a closer
look and I see the sweet coloured sky with marshmallow
clouds looking like I can jump up there I get out
my phone and take a pic

———

I escape looking towards the sunset, I see the
beautiful combinations of the colours in the sky, I
look into the clouds they look like marshmallows. I
sit on the grass and admire the sunset, I feel calm and
enjoying what I'm looking towards.

Isaac Miller

It's been one month since you left us. The Last Time I saw you was about four months ago. When I saw you I didn't think you would leave so soon. I've been listening to your favourite tune. One of my favourite lines out of it is *I hope you learn to make it on your own and if you love yourself just know you will never be alone.* As I think of that you put a smile on everyone's face when they were down even if we had a frown. The first time I met you was when I was about nine or ten at the skate park you loved riding scooters and then I stopped riding about twelve. Then at age of fifteen I started riding again it was only four months ago I saw you and I didn't think that would of been my last goodbye when I saw on the news that the teenager had a car crash I didn't think it was you then I saw on Facebook it was you and I burst into tears. #RideInPeaceNick <3 now every time I skate I ride for you. I remember that day when the back of your scooter deck broke, you were trying to snap it more and we all cracking up laughing. You were just so funny no-one can replace an angel like you love you Nick <3

www.sweatshop.ws